Cybersecurity and Decision Makers

Cybersecurity and Decision Makers

Data Security and Digital Trust

Marie de Fréminville

WILEY

First published 2020 in Great Britain and the United States by ISTE Ltd and John Wiley & Sons, Inc.

ISTE Ltd
27-37 St George's Road
London SW19 4EU
UK

www.iste.co.uk

John Wiley & Sons, Inc.
111 River Street
Hoboken, NJ 07030
USA

www.wiley.com

Library of Congress Control Number: 2019956830

British Library Cataloguing-in-Publication Data
A CIP record for this book is available from the British Library
ISBN 978-1-78630-519-0

Contents

Foreword

Directors and executives are now at the heart of cybersecurity issues. This is my conviction; this is my experience gained by launching one of the first cybersecurity companies in 2005 and by meeting many executives. This is my conviction as the director of a defense company that is particularly exposed to these risks, as well as active in the development of new protection strategies.

Let us make this expertise a driving force for differentiating our companies and France as a safe place to do business. This is where this book written by Marie de Fréminville takes on its full importance.

It brings together five years of work and exchanges between experts and leaders, between the State and industrial actors who forge our conviction that the issue of cybersecurity can no longer remain confined to the circles of geeks, but that it has become a real issue of economic resilience.

The issue is obviously much broader, and corporate governance must address it in all its dimensions: economic resilience, vulnerability of extended business strategies, customer protection, human issues, infrastructure development, insurance policy, crisis management, etc.

The general management and its board of directors must not only be aware of this, but must also each act according to its own responsibility, in order to set up the necessary organizations, risk governance, as well as the company's protection systems. It is this "call to consciences" that must resonate with the reader, who must then find appropriate solutions: this book will provide you with possible solutions and will enlighten you on the risks to be taken into account to inform your decisions.

As they say in the shift changeover: now it's up to you to take care of it...

Hervé GUILLOU
President and Chief Executive Officer
Naval Group

Preface

The organization of round tables with HEC Gouvernance and workshops with the Swiss Women Directors' Circle (*Cercle Suisse des Administratrices*) was the starting point of this book for decision makers: managers and directors of companies, public organizations, foundations or associations.

The protection of the company's strategic data and information systems is the responsibility of the directors and executives, as well as the company's decision makers, within the operational and functional departments, inside and outside the company.

The comments of the various speakers at these round tables have been included in this book.

In October 2016, "Understanding and preventing cyber-risks: a priority":

– Hervé Guillou, President and Chief Executive Officer of Naval Group;

– Alain Juillet, Director of Intelligence at the DGSE, Senior Manager for Economic Intelligence at the SGDSN and President of the CDSE (*Club des directeurs de sécurité et de sûreté des entreprises*);

– Guillaume Poupard, Director General of ANSSI (*Agence nationale de la sécurité des systèmes d'information*);

– Alain Bouillé, President of CESIN (*Club des experts de la sécurité de l'information et du numérique*);

– Alexandre Montay, Secretary General of METI (*Mouvement des entreprises de taille intermédiaire*).

In June 2017, "Cyber-risk: a subject to govern":

– Yves Bigot, General Manager of TV5 Monde;

– Brigitte Bouquot, President of AMRAE (*Association pour le management des risques et des assurances de l'entreprise*);

– Frédérick Douzet, Professor of Universities at the IFG (French Institute of Geopolitics) of the University of Paris 8 and Castex Chair in Cyberstrategy;

– Solange Ghernaouti, Professor of Information Security at UNIL (*université de Lausanne*) and Director of the Swiss Cyber Security Advisory and Research Group;

– Philippe Gaillard, Director of Technical and Cyber-risks at Axa France;

– Alain Robic, Partner Enterprise Risks and Services at Deloitte – Information Systems Security.

In December 2018, "Cybercrime and personal data protection: what good practices for the board of directors and managers?":

– Isabelle Falque-Pierrotin, President of the CNIL (*Commission nationale de l'informatique et des libertés*) since 2011, elected in 2017 in Hong Kong, President of the World Conference of Data Protection and Privacy Commissioners;

– Philippe Castagnac, President of the Management Board of Mazars, an international, integrated and independent organization specializing in audit, advice and accounting, tax and legal services;

– Annick Rimlinger, Executive Director of the CDSE (*Club des directeurs de sécurité et sûreté des entreprises*), founding member of Cercle K2 and member of the board of directors of Hack Academy;

– Éliane Rouyer, independent director, President of the Audit Committee and member of the Compensation Committee of Legrand, independent director of Vigéo Eiris.

I would like to thank all these speakers for their contributions and support, as well as Marc Triboulet (my teammate from HEC Gouvernance, with whom this round table cycle was initiated).

The training I developed within the Airbus group for directors and managers of subsidiaries, the work carried out for these conferences, as well as the exchanges during these round tables, have been supplemented by research work carried out over the past five years, participation in working groups (Switzerland's cybersecurity strategy, for example), support for several start-ups in the field of cybersecurity, the implementation of training, speeches given at the university of HEC Paris and Swiss management universities and at companies or service providers, the implementation of risk mapping, the definition and deployment of measures to improve compliance with the GDPR (General Data Protection Regulation), not to mention the implementation of cyber programs through companies, associations, foundations and public bodies.

Marie DE FRÉMINVILLE
December 2019

Introduction

Financial and Cyber Performance

Why not assess the cyber performance of companies in the same way as their financial and non-financial performance (governance and CSR – corporate social responsibility)?

Why not certify the cyber performance of companies in the same way as their financial performance via auditors, whose intervention is mandatory for companies of a certain size?

Despite some progress, the vast majority of shareholders, and therefore the board of directors and management, are primarily interested in the company's financial performance.

However, the digital age is introducing upheavals in the company and in its ecosystem. Indeed, the "all-digital" concerns all stakeholders, administration, public services and national and international infrastructures, defense and intelligence services.

We have reached a stage of non-return, which offers important opportunities, but which is also a source of fragility and major risks, particularly because cyber threat actors are becoming more professional and have significant resources to defraud, spy and sabotage.

The risks for companies are systemic: shareholders are financially exposed and directors, in charge of defining their strategy and ensuring their sustainability, are legally exposed if they do not inform themselves about the quality of data security and information system protection and if they do not

xviii   Cybersecurity and Decision Makers

ensure that an organization, procedures and tools for a high level of cybersecurity are in place.

There is no such thing as zero risk, but the negligence of a board of directors would be associated with it if no action were taken in the field of cybersecurity of the company and if the attacks had significant consequences for its proper functioning, profitability and reputation.

Financial performance should therefore no longer be the only priority. Financial performance and cyber performance should now be the two priorities of corporate governance bodies.

Should we therefore reinvent the governance body designated by the national actions, namely its competences, its functioning, its agenda and its partners?

For 50 years, we have been wading through a technological tsunami:

– 1970: mainframe;

– 1980: PC (Personal Computer) and client/server;

– 1990: Internet and e-commerce;

– 2000–2010: mobile and cloud;

– 2010–2020: Internet of Things and artificial intelligence;

– 2020–2030: quantum computing and blockchain.

The digital world is borderless and immaterial, and the threats are invisible.

Digital and related new technologies are transforming the way companies operate and business models.

The main cyber-risks are risks of malfunctioning of the industrial or commercial process, financial risks, as well as risks of loss of considerable confidential information (strategic information, personal information) which affect different sectors: hospitals, autonomous cars, banks, telecom operators, energy, etc., with potential human consequences.

According to a study conducted in the United States by the National Archives and Records Administration in 2018, 93% of companies that lost their data for 10 or more days declared bankruptcy in the year of the disaster and half (50%) filed for bankruptcy immediately after the attack.

The question is not "when will we be attacked?" but "what can we do to protect the company as much as possible, what can we do in the event of an attack, what can we do to restore systems as quickly as possible?"

Cyber-risk is an integral part of companies and also of personal organizations (everyone is concerned individually and as a member of an organization). It is not just a technical risk.

People are the weakest (and strongest) link in the entire safety chain.

This book does not deal with tools (hardware, software, servers, architecture), but with organizations, processes and behaviors, without which the company cannot improve its performance, security, incident or crisis management, and resilience.

It is about companies exercising their digital responsibility and maintaining or improving the trust of their stakeholders: customers, suppliers, partners and investors.

Only 30 years ago, I experienced the arrival of personal computers (computers and word processing existed, but were not deployed in companies), the digitization of financial operations (accounting, cost accounting, banking relations and cash management, tax returns, reporting tools, accounting and management consolidation, financial relations with customers and suppliers), as well as the digitization of human resources management (payroll, social declarations, recruitment, training), internal and external communication, particularly with the arrival of social networks, production (connected factories and extended companies), marketing and sales of course, and logistics.

All company functions are now concerned, as well as the relations with all stakeholders: customers, suppliers, service providers, subcontractors, shareholders (individual investors, investment funds), board of directors, auditors, employees, subsidiaries, proxy advisers (governance advisers who publicly comment on the proposals made by companies for their general meetings).

Companies are completely digitalized: their data, operations, accounts, processes are intangible; their internal and external communications, their products are connected.

Organizations and work habits have changed, skills have evolved, tools have been transformed, the classification of documents and people has sometimes (often?) fallen into oblivion.

Companies have been able to internationalize, thanks to the ultra-fast means of communication. We talk to the company across the street as well as to those in the United States or China: only the time difference is incompressible.

Companies share their data with their customers, suppliers, employees, shareholders, subsidiaries, etc. The digital environment provides companies with opportunities to create new businesses, new products and services and new customers, in order to optimize their organizations, reduce their costs, improve their internal and external processes, with their suppliers, service providers, subcontractors, investors, customers, depending on the business sector in which they operate.

Companies are judged on their financial performance: their accounts, their results, their balance sheet, their cash position, their share price, their growth and earnings potential, their non-financial performance (their governance and their social and environmental performance), but...

What about their cyber performance? Data governance, data security: integrity, confidentiality and accessibility, protection of the personal data they collect, use and archive, protection of computer systems that allow the exchange, storage and modification of these data.

A company may be financially successful, but a failure of its IT system or digital security can seriously affect its ability to sell or produce, to pay its suppliers, to exchange with its subcontractors and thus degrade its financial results, its reputation and the confidence of shareholders and stakeholders.

Cyber-risks are not the prerogative of a handful of specialists in the company but affect overall governance. In addition to the regulatory obligations regarding data security, it is a matter of protecting the company against the risk of loss of value, linked, for example, to the dissemination of confidential information.

"All connected, all committed, all responsible" is the slogan communicated by Guillaume Poupard, ANSSI's Director General at FIC 2019[1], from top to bottom and from bottom to top of private or public organizations: the board of directors, the executive committee and all the teams.

The trade war between major powers is more media-intensive than cyberwarfare, which is a weapon widely used by States, terrorist and criminal organizations, or corporations (spying). In addition, data collection is at the heart of the digital economy of the 21st Century, built around data valorization. This economy is currently dominated by the American and Chinese Internet giants. Finally, cybercriminals exploit the many vulnerabilities of digital tools, the human vulnerabilities generated by organizations that have not adapted, processes that have not been updated and collaborators that have not been trained.

There are cyberdeaths among the victims. Cyber-silence is a barrier to awareness. Finally, there are too many executives and directors burying their heads in the sand.

---

1 11th edition of the International Cybersecurity Forum (FIC).

An Increasingly Vulnerable World

1.1. The context

1.1.1. *Technological disruptions and globalization*

Technological disruptions are mostly digital in nature: automated knowledge, networks of connected objects, advanced robotics, 3D printing, cloud computing (85% of companies store data in a cloud; this practice is becoming more commonplace), mobile Internet, autonomous vehicles.

Until 2011, digital risks, or cyber-risks, did not appear in the World Economic Forum's major risk ranking.

According to the 2019 World Economic Forum study, technology will play a fundamental role in the risk landscape over the next decade, including data theft (personal data, data from companies, public organizations and governments), identity theft and cyber-attacks, as well as deadly "bugs", as shown by the Boeing 737 MAX crashes. According to the *Washington Post*, several flaws were discovered in the software of the aircraft's flight system. The preliminary investigation report on the Ethiopian Airlines crash clearly blames this accident on a failure of the MCAS stall protection system, which had already been identified in the Lion Air accident five months earlier. Not only was the information sent by the probes incorrect, but it was not possible for the pilots to take control of the aircraft.

This accident shows the risks of technological or digital failures, as well as the need to have them tested and certified by independent authorities. It also shows that digital accidents are not necessarily the result of attacks, but of human failures (programming, man–machine link, processes, organization): tools often have "good backs".

Cyberspace consists of computer equipment (computers, networks, connected objects, servers, printers, routers, etc.), software, applications, information systems and all information exchanged or stored via digital tools. It is the development of connections and flows that make security issues major issues, whether for States, companies or citizens.

In your company, has digital transformation had an impact on information systems and data security? Base: group (174 respondents)

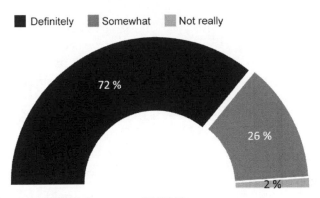

98 %

estimate that the digital transformation has
had **an impact on information systems**
and data security

No significant statistical change vs. 01/2018

Figure 1.1. *The impact of digital transformation on the security of information systems in all companies (source: according to CESIN). For a color version of this figure, see www.iste.co.uk/defreminville/cybersecurity.zip*

A number of technical black spots are at the root of data leaks:

– the totally decentralized structure of the Internet, based on a multitude of different networks (at the beginning of June "Swisscom's data passed through China", the customers of the Dutch operator KDN, as well as those of the French operators Bouygues and Numéricable, were also affected, according to the newspaper *Le Temps* on June 12, 2019);

– the architecture of IP addresses and domain names;

– the "backdoors" of the equipment;

– irregularities in the design of telecom operators' services;

– insufficient cryptographic tools for software and equipment.

1.1.2. *Data at the heart of industrial productivity*

With industry technologies 4.0 – ERP (Enterprise Resource Planning), CRM (Customer Relationship Management), 3D printing, extended enterprise – with digital marketing technologies – websites, cookies, tag management – or with connected products and security cameras, data has been put at the heart of activities. Many data are collected and recorded in computer systems and software by different departments, without the company having detailed knowledge of all data flows and mapping.

Understanding the geography of flows and mastering data is a fundamental strategic challenge for the competitiveness of companies, as well as for our defense capability.

Reliable information and the verification of digital identities are critical for companies, users and IT service providers.

1.1.3. *Cyberspace, an area without boundaries*

Hackers are difficult to identify, and there is a real asymmetry between attackers, who have many and effective weapons, despite few resources, and targets who have much greater resources, but who do not guarantee perfect defense.

Cybersecurity is about the security and digital sovereignty of every State, every company and every citizen. It is of major political, economic and social importance and must therefore be addressed from different angles: educational, legal and regulatory, social, technical, military, organizational, individual and collective (national and international).

The consequences of some attacks can be critical: for example, the attack on the SWIFT interbank network between April and May 2016, which led to fraudulent misappropriations of several tens of millions of dollars in Bangladesh, or the denial of service attack of October 21, 2016 on Dyn servers (a service that allows the users of a dynamic IP address to access a domain name), which paralyzed part of the Internet network in the United States for several hours and seriously disrupted the economic activities concerned.

1.1.4. *IT resources*

Comprehensive knowledge of IT tools (hardware, software, network) is a structural challenge for companies: the way they have developed and managed their IT infrastructures in recent decades – fragmentary, in *silos*, at a time when risks were low – makes it more difficult for them to supervise them globally, which is essential for effective cybersecurity management.

1.2. Cybercrime

1.2.1. *The concept of cybercrime*

In short, it refers to criminal acts in the context of new technologies. We are also talking about computer fraud. Cybercrime includes, among other things, the illegal acquisition of private, personal or sensitive information. Cybercrime includes all crimes whose preparation or execution involves electronic data processing systems, such as sabotage, espionage and data interception.

Cyberspace offers criminal opportunities: digital services and infrastructures are a gateway to malicious intent. Any connected equipment is hackable; it is necessary to ensure continuity between physical security and cybersecurity.

As for computer attacks, or cyber-attacks, every week, new cases are revealed by the press, on all continents, in all sectors of activity (industry, banking, hospitals, hotels, online sales, etc.), for all types of companies: from start-ups to large listed groups, any other entities such as associations, foundations, town halls, public administrations and infrastructures, or even connected objects (surveillance cameras, pacemakers, children's toys). And the press only reveals the tip of the iceberg. There is a veil of silence on the part of companies, which is understandable: none of them want to divulge their difficulties and especially not their cyber weaknesses.

Computer instabilities or intrusions are made possible both by the increasing integration of new technologies into all aspects of our lives (mobility, home automation, purchasing, travel, banking, etc.) and into the lives of companies (sales, production, communication, security, financial operations, administration, customer relations, suppliers, employees, investors, banks, etc.) and encouraged by the digitization of public services, as well as by the increasing sophistication of computer attacks.

Although information systems are increasingly protected, allowing more attacks to be blocked (in number and percentage), the number of intrusions was stable in 2018 compared to 2017, according to an Accenture study.

As the graph in Figure 1.2 illustrates, computer attacks are not a new phenomenon; they started more than 30 years ago, with the birth of computer networks and then the Internet.

They have then intensified due to the increase in vulnerabilities related to the digitization of economic operations, the opening up of computer networks, data exchanges, mobility, the development of applications and connected objects, and the widespread networking of computers.

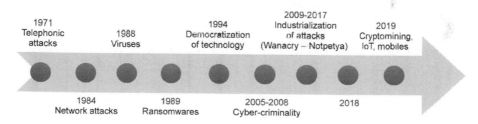

Figure 1.2. *History (source: Starboard Advisory)*

It should be noted that hardware and software are sometimes sold voluntarily with "backdoors", which allow software developers or hardware manufacturers to use them to monitor or even take control of the software's activities, or to take control of the computer. It is like a house builder selling you a house while keeping the key to a hidden door.

These backdoors make it possible to carry out maintenance operations efficiently or to disable the software in the event of disagreement with its customer (non-payment of license).

They can also be installed by hackers to copy or destroy valuable data (IDs, passwords, social security numbers, bank details, means of payment, confidential information) or take control of a computer and use it to carry out malicious actions (computer viruses, denial of service, ransom demands, etc.).

Attackers organize and specialize: some open the door to allow others to break in and take the data or organize financial fraud. The service provided (open the door) is sold at auction on the darknet.

Finally, on this backdoor issue, States have different opinions. Russia has legislated to provide publishers with a way to access encrypted communications. The member states of the Five Eyes alliance (intelligence services of the United States, Australia, New Zealand, the United Kingdom and Canada) also wish to impose the introduction of software vulnerabilities.

The main and official objective is to be able to decipher certain communications that could be linked to terrorist activities and to share information between intelligence services. It also allows State spying, access to trade secrets and the infringement of individual freedoms. The risk is that these vulnerabilities may be exploited by malicious people.

Digital trust therefore depends on the ability of companies to protect systems and data, as well as on the protection of the entire ecosystem, including digital strategies put in place by governments and the work undertaken by information system security agencies to ensure the protection of equipment, applications, networks and software.

1.2.2. *Five types of threats*

The National Cybersecurity Agency of France (ANSSI) identified five major cyber threat trends observed in France and Europe in 2018.

Some sectors of activity, considered unlikely targets, are now being targeted. This is the case, for example, for the agri-food sector, which means that no company is immune, according to Guillaume Poupard, ANSSI's Director General.

During the night of April 10–11, 2019, Fleury Michon (a mid-sized, family-owned and independent company specializing in the preparation of deli meats, ready meals and fresh surimi) was hit by a computer virus. To avoid its spread, all systems were disconnected. The plants, as well as the logistics unit, were shut down on April 11. After analysis, appropriate security measures were deployed to allow the activity to restart on April 15.

The unit dedicated to culinary aids was relaunched the morning of April 16. "Our customers' orders have been delivered again since this morning. The impacts, which are currently being quantified, will be limited and covered by insurance taken out for this purpose", the company stated in a press release dated April 15, 2019.

1.2.2.1. *Cyber espionage*

Cyber espionage is the highest risk for organizations, according to ANSSI.

The attacks are highly targeted and technically sophisticated and increasingly target critical sectors of activity and specific critical national infrastructure, such as defense, health or research.

Guillaume Poupard mentioned, during his speech at the French Institute of Directors on April 17: "ten to twenty very serious cases per year. We don't talk about it, but these attacks exist. Their silence creates a perception bias!" he says.

The best way to access confidential information today is through a computer attack. Victims discover the attacks, sometimes by chance, sometimes by third parties, sometimes thanks to ANSSI. Sometimes, victims discover the attack five years later. The managers then discovered that all their emails could be read. The average time to discover an attack is about a 100 days; it has decreased, but it is still important. Meanwhile, the pirates are taking action.

Cyber espionage is gradually eroding the value of companies and even destabilizing some of them: it is large-scale economic spying using cyber infiltration techniques to steal the most valuable assets (strategic files, business proposals, managers' email boxes, etc.). Eighty percent of the value of Fortune 500 companies is made up of industrial property and other intangible assets, and cyber espionage is a perfect way to access them.

TeamViewer is one of the world's leading suppliers of software for the remote control of computers and servers. It was the victim of user account diversions, reported by many customers as originating from Chinese IP addresses, and reportedly infected with Winnti malware in late 2016, as well as German steel producer ThyssenKrupp and pharmaceutical giant Bayer, which acknowledged a hacking attack in 2018, during which the Winnti malware program was also deployed.

1.2.2.2. *Indirect attacks*

Indirect attacks increased significantly in 2018, according to ANSSI. As large companies are more secure, attackers target suppliers or service providers, who are more vulnerable, to reach their final targets. When it comes to an IT service provider, it is difficult to distinguish whether the connections come from the service provider or from an attacker who has broken into the service provider's premises. Through this partner or service provider, it is possible to enter several of its customers' premises.

It is therefore essential to carefully select suppliers, to contract security requirements and to audit the level of protection of their IT systems, their organization, employee training, as well as their security policy and processes.

1.2.2.3. *Sabotage*

These operations are deployed in the political arena, as well as in the corporate sector. They increased significantly in 2018. They are not necessarily sophisticated, but make the service of their target unavailable and can go as far as sabotage.

Some of these attacks can be likened to acts of war or terrorism. It is therefore a matter of national security and resilience: given the purpose of these attacks (governmental organizations and vital operators), they generally target products and/or services that are vital to the nation. The attack, attributed to Russia, on Estonia's banking infrastructure in 2007, is a first concrete event. Since then, Stuxnet, Aramco and TV5 Monde have been more recent examples.

1.2.2.4. *Cryptojacking or cryptocurrency mining*

This type of cyber-attack consists of using the power of the victim's computer to undermine cryptocurrency.

In 2018, many such attacks were observed: increasingly organized attackers were taking advantage of security breaches to compromise their targets' equipment, by depositing cryptomarket miners without their victims' knowledge.

1.2.2.5. *Online fraud and cybercrime*

Online fraud is a permanent cyber threat, both for companies and large organizations and for individuals. Large companies are better protected: they invest, detect and protect themselves.

The attackers then turn to less exposed but more vulnerable targets, such as local authorities or health sector actors, who were thus the targets of numerous *phishing* attacks in 2018.

A recent and emblematic example of the exceptional reactivity of cybercriminals: the burning of Notre-Dame on April 15, 2019, the State set up a site to collect donations from individuals, with a view to reconstruction.

This is a good opportunity for fraudsters, the money will flow. With a fake *"Fondation du Patrimoine"* logo, but with a real RIB (bank account details), an email urged the "friends of France" to make donations for a "symbol of our history". The site (created in Italy) was fraudulent and tried to surf the wave of generosity. It is not the only initiative; other scams have been identified and reported.

1.2.3. *Five types of attackers*

1.2.3.1. *Looking for easy money*

Targets are identified according to two main criteria: they have assets (data with a *darknet* value or good financial performance) and they are fragile from the point of view of protecting IT systems and/or internal organization and procedures.

1.2.3.2. Cyberactivists/hacktivists

The best-known cyberactivist or hacktivist movement is the Anonymous movement, created in 2006, better known since 2008, which is looking for hackers because of the principle of anonymity, lack of hierarchy and freedom of expression. The most common type of hacktivist attack is the degradation of websites, in order to insert a political message.

Anonymous launches denial of service (DoS) attacks against the sites of targeted companies, considered as enemies of the values defended by the movement. In December 2010, attacks were carried out on the MasterCard site following MasterCard's decision to no longer provide services to WikiLeaks, a non-governmental organization founded by Julian Assange in 2006, whose objective is to publish documents, some of which are confidential, as well as political and social analyses on a global scale. Its purpose is to give an audience to alerters and information leaks, while protecting its sources. Several million documents relating to corruption, spying and human rights violation scandals involving dozens of countries around the world have been published on the website since its inception.

In late 2010 and early 2011, the group was involved in attacks against countries with high levels of Internet censorship.

On April 2, 2011, Anonymous launched an operation called "#opsony" against Sony and the PlayStation Network, to denounce the legal proceedings against hackers who had managed to bypass the digital protections of the PlayStation.

This type of activist movement attacks may not have a direct financial impact, but might have a significant media impact and therefore an impact that seriously damages the company's reputation, as well as the reputation of its officers and directors.

1.2.3.3. Competitors (or States) for the purpose of espionage or sabotage

Cyber espionage is very common, and small- and medium-sized enterprises (SMEs) are not immune.

Ruag, a Swiss armaments and defense systems company, owned by the confederation, like other companies, is the target of computer attacks and has been infiltrated by malware for months. "According to initial evidence, the cyber-spyware attack on Ruag began in December 2014", said Renato Kalbermatten, spokesman for the Federal Department of Defense.

According to press reports, the cyber-attack on Ruag allowed hackers to access tens of thousands of pieces of sensitive information. MELANI, the Reporting and Analysis Centre for Information Assurance of the Swiss Confederation, describes this sophisticated cyber-attack in the technical report published on its website, melani.admin.ch.

Here is an excerpt from the report:

> The Swiss Federal Council has decided to publish this report to enable organizations to detect the presence of similar infections on their networks and highlight the attackers' modus operandi. The attackers were very patient during the infiltration and lateral movement. They only addressed the targets of interest to them, using various measures (list of target IPs and complete digital fingerprint before and after initial infection). After entering the network, they made lateral movement by infecting other devices and obtaining higher privileges. One of their main targets was the Active Directory, which allowed them to control other devices and access data of interest to them using the rights and membership of the appropriate groups. The malware used IITTP to transfer the data to the outside.

1.2.3.4. *Employees: the most frequent threat*

The threat may come from employees responsible for improper handling, which is not necessarily malicious: sending information to a recipient other than the one who was supposed to receive the information (the employee is sometimes a senior manager, in a hurry, stressed, inattentive).

It is sometimes harmless, sometimes serious, and, in any case, it is not ideal for image and reputation. Training (especially during recruitment), awareness and vigilance are key factors. But tools are not everything.

The threat can come from careless employees: they are not really malicious, but they do not feel concerned about the information they are handling or the protection of their company. They are not "committed" and may not be sufficiently supervised. There is a responsibility on the part of managers and executives to implement rules and tools that prevent mistakes, as well as a culture to develop to improve employee engagement.

It can come from untrained employees who will not have the necessary vigilance: recruitment manager who opens a CV, sent by a fake candidate (it is necessary to ensure the origin but it is sometimes difficult, and attacks are increasingly sophisticated), director/president who receives a fake update from his Wikipedia, and who hastily opens it to read the public information about him/her.

It can come from malicious employees: sending files outside, clicking on a malicious email and opening doors with the complicity of the outside world.

Finally, it can come from employees who are victims of blackmail; the excellent detective novel *Tension extrême* explains very well how intrusions succeed, even in ultra-secure environments, thanks to the exploitation of human weaknesses or oversized egos.

In any case, it will be the coherence of the mechanisms, tools, organization, procedures, training and commitment that will make it possible to resist attacks.

1.2.3.5. *The States*

The main subject of this book is not cyberwarfare, but it can have considerable impacts on companies (it already has several times). The cyber conflict is changing the geopolitical landscape, and it is to be taken into account in corporate strategy.

The cyber war between States is no longer a secret and is the subject of many publications and declarations. The French Minister of Defense, Florence Parly, publicly presented, for the first time on January 18, 2019, the framework of France's offensive computer warfare doctrine, and made a statement that could largely apply to companies.

Here are some excerpts from this statement, which marks a change in the stance of States:

Stolen data. Spy mailboxes. Looted servers and disrupted information systems. Cyberspace has become a place of confrontation like any other. A place where thousands of hackers advance undetected. A place of impunity where some nations hide to attack better. A place of immense violence, which can permanently block us.

Let us recall WannaCry, which reached 150 countries, stations and industries. A few days ago, let us remember the thousands of data from the German political class that were hacked and revealed.

Thinking they are protected by the anonymity of their keyboards, some individuals, groups and states believe they can do anything. Their codes, 'logic bombs' and other malwares have very real effects.

This phenomenon is getting worse [...]. And we probably haven't seen anything yet. While attacks may have affected physical infrastructure in Ukraine or Iran, they have not yet succeeded in causing massive and lasting damage to economies and societies. Our military systems are also being spied on, targeted and attacked.

At the end of 2017, abnormal connections on the Ministry of the Armed Forces' Internet mail server were noted. After analysis, these connections revealed that an attacker was seeking direct access to the contents of the mailboxes of nineteen ministry officials, including those of a few sensitive personalities. Without our vigilance, our entire fuel supply chain for the French Navy would have been exposed.

In 2018, more than two security events per day affected our ministry, our operations, our technical expertise and even an army training hospital. Some are the result of malicious groups. Others from isolated hackers. But some of them come from States.

In 2017, the Cyber Defence Command was created. In perfect coordination with the National Agency for Information Systems Security (ANSSI), the Ministry of the Armed Forces is taking responsibility for cybersecurity. This effort only makes sense if it is collective. Cyber defense is not a matter for specialists but for everyone.

All attacks are international in scope. Every company, every partner in the defense world has a role to play. Our opponents take every opportunity to reach us; this of course involves manufacturers, their subcontractors, their suppliers, their employees. The more the department strengthens its firewalls, the more individuals and manufacturers are targeted. Every weapon system, every computer, every smartphone, and tomorrow every connected object, can, without the owner's knowledge, be not only a target, but a vector of cyber-attacks. This is one of the reasons why we believe in SMEs and start-ups, because they will be at the heart of our digital success.

Cybersecurity must be taken into account from the design stage in each weapon, information and communication system. Cyber hygiene is not a luxury, it is an absolute necessity for our weapon systems throughout their life cycle, from their technical design to their operational use.

In the event of a cyber-attack against our forces, we reserve the right to retaliate, in accordance with the law, by the means and at the time of our choice. We also reserve the right to neutralize the effects and digital means used, regardless of the attacker.

Today, France chooses to fully equip itself with cyber weapons for its military operations. We consider the cyber weapon as an operational weapon in its own right. It is a necessary choice, in terms of responsibility. We will use it proportionately, but those who are tempted to attack our armed forces should know that we will not be afraid to use it.

The French Minister has expressed herself so clearly because the cyber threat is a serious one, for States, businesses and citizens alike. The cyberspace created by the United States in 1989, whose stated objective was to improve the sharing of fluid information and communications across a borderless and collaborative world, has gradually evolved into an area marked by the growth of cybercrime in all its forms.

Cybercrime is expected to cost $6 trillion in 2021, up from $3 trillion in 2015, and will be more profitable than the global trade in illegal drugs.

Invited to a conference on cybersecurity organized by the Ministry of the Economy and Finance and the Banque de France, as part of France's G7 presidency, Denis Kessler, CEO of the reinsurance company Scor, said that "the reinsurance industry believes that cyber-risk is as important as the risk of natural disasters. This gives an idea of the magnitude of the threat we face".

The establishment of governance of the digital space is therefore essential, such as data protection, the creation of a digital identity, which would make it possible, in particular, to identify criminals, the establishment of standards and rules concerning the content of published information and digital privacy.

1.3. The cybersecurity market

1.3.1. *The size of the market and its evolution*

The cybersecurity market (hardware, software and services) is still small: it currently represents less than 2% of global GDP (estimated at 120 billion), but it has been growing strongly: +10% per year since 2016, and according to Cybersecurity Ventures forecasts, it is expected to grow by 15–20% from 2019 to 2021, due to the rapid development of corporate digitization, as well as due to the growth in regulations: personal data protection, obligation to respect international standards and sectoral regulations.

Technologies are constantly evolving, and the development of artificial intelligence, Big Data and cloud computing is forcing players to quickly renew solutions.

Hackers are perfecting their methods and tools, forcing companies, their IT providers and all cybersecurity actors to constantly improve their solutions to defend themselves more effectively.

1.3.2. *The market by sector of activity*

The cybersecurity market has developed unevenly across sectors. The 2018 report by IDC (International Data Corporation) indicates that three sectors will increase their investments in 2019: banks, industry and governments (administrations).

The telecommunications sector will become the fourth largest sector in terms of IT security investments by 2022.

In France, the IT security market is expected to grow by an average of 8% per year between 2017 (2.6 billion) and 2021 (3.6 billion) and represent 6.5% of the IT market in 2021, compared to 5.2% in 2017.

This is a young market, with a multitude of suppliers. Cybersecurity fairs are full of recently created suppliers. For cybersecurity managers and IT service providers, the offer is wide, too wide. Be careful about the compatibility of solutions, or rather the incompatibility of solutions; also, be careful about "miracle" solutions, which are expensive and do not protect you. Finally, even if you have an excellent quality (and therefore expensive) armored door and highly sophisticated locks, if you open the door to just anyone, the strength of your door will not be very useful.

Security is based on a system that includes tools, organizations, procedures and skills, and therefore training.

The consolidation of the many suppliers is inevitable. Large companies that have invested heavily will enter a phase of optimization, rationalization and centralization of purchasing, to avoid dispersion and additional costs, while improving the efficiency of the systems.

1.3.3. *Types of purchases and investments*

Solutions dedicated to monitoring and protecting information systems (including SOCs, Security Operation Centers), internally or externally, will represent the main investment for organizations this year. The second area of investment will be network security equipment (firewalls, intrusion detection and prevention technologies). The increase in massive data leaks and Advanced Persistent Threat (APT) attacks are the main reasons for organizations to deploy defensive and proactive solutions. Finally, companies will also rely on integration services and security software for fixed and mobile terminals.

This market, which is still in its infancy, is currently being organized, particularly by type of business: cloud offers, audit, training, services, certification and inspection, intelligence, etc.

1.3.4. *Geographical distribution*

In terms of geographical distribution, 40% of the world market is currently in the United States and 25% in Europe, according to an IDC (International Data Corporation) study.

China is the second largest market. Expenditure on security by the State (or local governments), telecommunications and central government accounts for 45% of the total.

Japan and the United Kingdom are the other two most important markets.

Two-thirds of IT security spending in 2019 is expected to come from large companies.

1.4. Cyber incidents

1.4.1. *The facts*

Remember that a computer incident or accident is not necessarily linked to an attack or hacking. Indeed, the causes are diverse, malicious or accidental, internal or external. A fire or flood will affect the information systems or data of the company or client companies (if the company hosts its customers' data), with the same impacts, which can be significant, as a computer attack.

Physical security and computer security are therefore closely linked. Nevertheless, given the digitization of organizations and the opening up of information systems to the outside world, cybercrime is growing exponentially and is indeed a major new source of risk. According to Cybersecurity Ventures, a company will be the victim of a ransom every 11 seconds by 2021.

Cyber-attacks currently affect 2 billion people, and Microsoft estimates that the number of people affected will double by 2021 to 4 billion.

1.4.1.1. *Information on cybercrime*

Many studies are published weekly by consulting firms, cybersecurity providers or clubs of security managers, IT managers or IT security managers.

These studies have several biases:

– some are oriented toward commercial purposes (selling products or services) or political purposes (empowering actors);

– the samples on which the survey is carried out are reduced in comparison to the overall economic sector;

– the answers are declarative; the surveys are sometimes the result of telephone surveys;

– the interviewees, although there is a promise of confidentiality from the investigators, do they know/say the reality of the facts about the number of attacks, their severity, the success of the intrusions or the origin of the incidents?

– in general, most companies are not ready to provide information about their vulnerabilities, computer incidents, fraud or data theft, and that is understandable. This is quite logical; how can customers, shareholders, suppliers and bankers trust a company whose computer systems are malfunctioning and which can no longer sell, produce or communicate?

– companies often do not file complaints: either because of confidentiality concerns and/or because they do not expect support from the police, who will be unable to trace the origin of the attack, or because of a lack of competent resources or because the means to be implemented are disproportionate.

The quality of the information is nevertheless improving, thanks to

– regulations and obligations to report data leaks to the CNIL or ICO (as part of the GDPR, General Data Protection Regulation), or to customers depending on the nature of the data that has been removed from the company;

– declarations to ANSSI (National Cybersecurity Agency of France), which are also listed and reported annually;

– a source of improvement in the quality of information represented by insurance (insurance companies and brokers). Indeed, insurance companies are developing their cyber-risk coverage offers, although this is a difficult market, given the weak history and the difficulty of estimating risks. More companies are studying the extension of their insurance policies to cyber-risks, and incident data are more reliable, even if the insurance companies themselves are discreet about the outcome of incidents.

What is more annoying is when executives hide the truth from themselves, or when they hide the situation from their shareholders and board of directors. "We were attacked, we went through the crisis, back to business". We could call them "cyber avoiders".

The press does not necessarily need to know, but the board of directors and shareholders must be informed when the impacts are significant and the risks threaten the company's sustainability.

Suppliers, experts who work with their customers, insurance companies, audit firms and digital investigation firms (computer forensics, which use techniques specialized in the collection, identification, description, security, extraction, authentication, analysis, interpretation and explanation of digital information) have a relatively reliable view of trends: they hold factual information, which allows them to extrapolate the origins of incidents, impacts and developments.

1.4.1.2. *The origin of the threats*

The main causes of computer incidents are as follows:

– a system user: most of the time, he or she does not want to compromise the integrity of the system, but his or her behavior promotes danger;

– a malicious individual: he or she enters the system, legitimately or not, and accesses data or programs to which he or she is not supposed to have access (via software used within the system, but not properly secured, for example);

– malicious software: software designed to harm or abuse system resources is installed (inadvertently or maliciously) on the system, opening the door to intrusions or modifying data; confidential data may be collected without the user's knowledge and reused for malicious purposes;

– a disaster (theft, fire, water damage), caused by improper handling or malicious intent, results in the loss of equipment and/or data.

The figures published are frightening: a company is attacked every 40 seconds[1], 33% of ransom victims will not fully recover their data, 20% of paid victims will not recover their data either[2].

1.4.1.3. *Their implementation*

Organized crime is growing because it is profitable and low-risk: criminals are based in countries where their activities are neither monitored nor prosecuted.

What types of cyberattacks has your company encountered in the last 12 months?
Base: noticing an attack (139 respondents) several possible responses

Figure 1.3. *The five different types of attacks that companies face each year (source: according to CESIN)*

Ransom software

Imagine a burglar stealing all your company's sensitive files and promising to bring them back to you if you pay a ransom. This is the method

---

1 Source: https://www.kaspersky.fr/about/press-releases/2016_ransomware-kaspersky-lab-recense-une-attack-all-40-seconds-against-businesses-in-2016.
2 Source: *2017 Norton Cyber Security Insights Report Global Results*; https://www.symantec.com/content/dam/symantec/docs/about/2017-ncsir-global-results-en.pdf.

applied today with digital means. Files are not taken away, but encrypted, making them inaccessible.

Cyber-attack campaigns are global; data is encrypted by attackers (now well encrypted) and results in the loss of data from attacked companies or organizations, unless the backup system is not affected and the data can be restored without having to pay a ransom.

The ransoms requested are often low, and many customers pay because the amounts are lower than the impact resulting from the loss of data or the shutdown of their information systems. The State recommends not to pay, in particular, because it encourages cybercrime, but the pragmatism of companies usually leads to paying the ransom and restarting their activity as soon as possible, to be able to sell and produce, deliver to their customers and pay their suppliers.

Attackers, in most cases, decrypt the data once the ransom has been collected, allowing companies to continue their activities. Indeed, the attacked spread the good news to those who failed to restore their backups, via their IT service providers: "Trust the hackers. If you pay, they will give you back access to your data and computer systems".

However, it should be noted that, in most cases, ransomware can be decrypted to retrieve the data by a provider paid between €2,000 and €4,000, which is often much less than the amounts requested by cybercriminals.

Phishing

Studies show that between 70 and 90% of cyber-attacks, and resulting data leaks, start with "phishing", which means that employees who clicked on malicious emails are responsible for most successful attacks.

The figures vary from study to study, but the ranking is always the same in the causes cited by companies that have experienced computer incidents: fraudulent emails, data access, malware, loss or theft of computer equipment, fraud (embezzlement or scam) are the most common threats encountered. Attacks can be massive or targeted.

1.4.1.4. *The targets*

How many cyberattacks have you noticed in your company in the last 12 months?   :
Base: group (174 respondents)

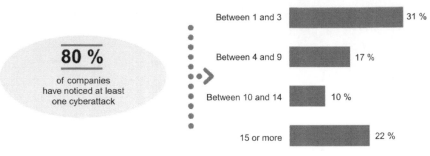

80 %

of companies
have noticed at least
one cyberattack

Between 1 and 3   31 %

Between 4 and 9   17 %

Between 10 and 14   10 %

15 or more   22 %

No significant statistical change vs. 01/2018

Figure 1.4. *Still a very high rate of companies affected*
by cyber-attacks (source: according to CESIN)

Cyber-risk is no longer a technical risk but a corporate, international risk, and also a risk for governments and public organizations. It is now an integral part of business reality, such as fire risk or building safety.

The cyber-risk landscape is constantly changing. Cyber-risks are complex and difficult to quantify, particularly because of the rapidly changing technological environment and the lack of historical data on cyber-claims.

Large companies, such as KPMG, Deloitte or Airbus, cities, political parties and even governments are also vulnerable and victims of attacks. Those who have prepared themselves are managing the crisis, communicating as little as possible, and avoiding leaks in the press.

All companies are potential victims, regardless of their size, activity or location, and come from a wide variety of backgrounds, as this sample of examples shows:

– the nuclear industry "is no exception"; "there have been cases of random malware attacks against nuclear power plants", said the Director General of the International Atomic Energy Agency (IAEA) in 2016;

– the space industry, via "ground attacks" on control centers, jamming of radio waves from a transmitter or receiver, data interception, takeover (information sent over the Internet via a satellite hijacked, copied, stolen or modified). On September 7, 2018, according to *Le Monde*, French Defense Minister Florence Parly revealed that the Russian satellite Luch-Olymp had approached a Franco-Italian satellite "a little too close" in 2017;

– In May 2019, *Le Parisien* announced that "Picoty SA, a company specializing in fuel distribution in the Creuse, a remote area in the center of France, was the victim of a ransom attack: the company's computer system was attacked by a file encryption system. Cybercriminals then demanded 500,000 euros so that the company could recover access to it";

– On June 14, 2019, according to AFP, a complaint about a cyber-attack on the ransom system was filed in the Zaventem police zone by Asco Industries, a Belgian subcontractor, in particular, of major manufacturers such as Airbus, Boeing, Bombardier and Lockheed Martin. The Belgian plant was closed for several days; the other sites in the United States, Canada and Germany were also shut down. "We are currently working hard to get our business up and running as quickly as possible and to serve our customers", said a company spokeswoman.

1.4.1.5. *The worst shoemakers in the world*

On April 17, 2019, the American company Verint, a leader in surveillance and cyber intelligence, operating mainly in Israel, was reportedly attacked by *ransomware*, while most of the leaders were attending a conference in Italy. The attack would have been identified very quickly and the security teams could have reacted quickly. No one is safe.

Le Canard enchaîné from February 13, 2019, revealed data leaks from CLUSIF (*Club des experts en sécurité informatique français*), which did not take the necessary precautions.

Indeed, more than 2,200 names and personal details (surnames, first names, email addresses, mobile phone number) of the main IT security directors and conference participants were freely accessible on the CLUSIF website.

This list included the contact details of the CISO (Chief Information Security Officer) of the Presidency of the Republic, as well as the contact details of officials of the Nuclear Safety Authority (NSA), experts from the Armed Forces Staff, Matignon, the Senate, arms manufacturers or banks, declares *Le Canard enchainné*.

To retrieve this list, all you had to do was search with the keywords "Clusif" and "csv". The file was hosted by CLUSIF, but not well protected. A common human error in website management.

To prevent the leakage of sensitive data, while compliance with security rules is essential, supervision by competent persons of the application of these standards is essential.

1.4.2. *Testimonials versus silence*

With the exception of Yves Bigot, CEO of TV5 Monde, who was attacked in 2015, few business leaders agreed to publicly testify about the crisis, the failures of its information systems, its processes, the training of its employees, the lack of awareness of the risks and consequences of an attack, the investments to be made, the discipline to be implemented and the budgets to be allocated.

Following these incidents, which almost cost TV5 Monde their livelihood, Yves Bigot spoke at numerous conferences. There is nothing like this testimony to understand the risks and put in place the necessary measures to avoid such a traumatic experience.

In France, there is also a "before Saint-Gobain" and "after Saint-Gobain". Pierre-André Chalendar, CEO of Saint-Gobain, did not publicly testify when this major French company was attacked.

On the other hand, he testified, confidentially, to the boards of directors and executive committees of CAC 40 companies so that the directors and officers could take up the subject. Testimonies are therefore rare, which is a pity, because they are effective.

Silence is the most common practice; it is detrimental to the divulgation of information that would allow for a better and faster response.

The clubs of IT safety or security managers are virtuous; they allow you to exchange, learn, progress and defend yourself better.

1.4.3. *Trends*

1.4.3.1. *Cybercriminal methods*

Cyber-attacks are improving and evolving. The attack surfaces are growing: mobility, cloud, connected objects and, at the same time, the ability of targets to monitor, detect and protect themselves from attackers are increasing.

Targets are therefore increasingly attacked often via their suppliers, subcontractors, partners and service providers: it has become more complicated to go through the door; so, the attacker will go through the window.

1.4.3.2. *The attackers*

Attackers are progressing; they are always one step ahead: cryptomining, IoT (Internet of Things) networks to launch attacks, APT (Advanced Persistent Threats) are the techniques recently developed to reach targets, their computer systems and data, destabilize (disclose customer IDs, passwords and personal data) and sabotage critical systems (industrial system shutdowns).

Targeting victims is now a priority over massive attacks. It is more lucrative and more efficient.

1.4.3.3. *Connected objects*

To raise awareness and encourage citizens in Japan to better protect themselves, the National Institute of Information and Communications Technology has tried to hack into citizens' connected objects, starting in February 2019: the organization will try to use default passwords and other basic passwords from dictionaries to try to infiltrate 200 million connected objects randomly selected from households across the country.

Initially, routers and webcams will be targeted. Thereafter, the government will attack the connected objects of the Smart Home.

Owners of successfully hacked devices will – in principle – be informed and asked to urgently change their passwords for more reliable identifiers. However, they will not be forced to do so. The initiative could be extended for the next five years.

1.4.3.4. *Cyberwarfare*

Spying and sabotage operations, as well as information warfare, are now carried out by digital means and are at the forefront of strategic action, as Jean-Louis Gergorin and Léo Isaac-Dognin explain in their book *Cyber. La guerre permanente*, published in 2018. They very clearly detail this new form of warfare: digital technology makes it possible to act at a distance and offers a paralyzing and reversible capability. Moreover, it considerably increases the global reach, instantaneous speed and power of intelligence, influence and clandestine action (difficulty of attribution) with a low cost (which significantly modifies the balances between major powers) and a high targeting capacity.

Cyberwarfare between States can impact not only governments but also sensitive public organizations and, more seriously, critical national infrastructure (energy, telecommunications, defense, etc.) and by extension (or directly) companies.

The alliance of 29 NATO member countries recognized cyberspace as a domain of war, as well as land, air and sea, in 2014. In late 2018, member countries declared that NATO would establish a cyberspace operations center to coordinate NATO's cyber activities. NATO also discussed integrating each country's IT capabilities into Alliance operations.

In September 2018, the White House warned foreign hackers that it would increase offensive measures as part of a new national cyber security strategy. US intelligence officials were expecting a series of digital attacks before the November 6 elections.

The United States announced in 2019 that it will use offensive and defensive IT capabilities on behalf of NATO.

1.4.4. *Examples*

1.4.4.1. *Information leaks*

Information leaks can be the result of misuse or negligence, including by managers, consultants or IT service providers: data are sent by mistake to one contact instead of another, database access management is unreliable, passwords are left visible, or easy to guess, passwords are not updated regularly, software is not updated, double authentication recommendations are not respected, confidential data is accessible, transferable and able to be copied. Websites are not secure either.

The company must therefore first govern its data: what data is collected, by whom, why, where it is stored, by whom?

How is the data classified, how confidential is it, who has access to it, who can modify it, who manages authorizations?

Data security therefore depends first and foremost on good data governance: who is responsible in the company, what are the rules, are the rules known and applied?

1.4.4.2. *Some examples of famous attacks*

The first attack: Wannacry

It struck in May and June 2017; it is a *ransomware* that has paralyzed hundreds of thousands of computers around the world, affecting the British healthcare system, German railways or Renault factories.

The attack is global. In more than 100 countries, a virus blocked computers until a ransom of $300–600 was paid in bitcoins. Fifty British hospitals (National Health Service) were partially paralyzed, telecommunications companies (Vodafone, Telefonica), the Romanian intelligence services, Renault and its assembly lines, the factories of the Honda automobile group in Japan, to name but a few.

In Germany, Deutsche Bahn was reached: on the screens displaying train timetables in German stations, the ransom request message was displayed.

The Wannacry virus made a lot of noise, had spectacular impacts, but did not allow the attackers to recover millions (30,000 dollars would have been recovered in France), mainly because of a poorly built payment system.

On the other hand, the costs to companies for restarting systems, replacing computers, hiring IT security experts and securing information systems to avoid becoming a victim again are much higher. Consolidated information is not available. In England, the estimated cost to hospitals is estimated at £90 million.

The second attack: NotPetya

This is an attack of destruction, sabotage. This malware deleted the files from the computers it was visiting, posing as *ransomware*. The main known French victim is Saint-Gobain, whose loss of earnings is estimated at 250 million euros. Its annual report indicates an impact of 80 million on operating income; the impact on non-recurring income is not quantified.

"The year was also marked by the cyber-attack of 27 June, to which the group was able to react very quickly to restore normal operational activities but also to strengthen its defenses. The impact on operating income for 2017 is estimated at €80 million:

> Overall, about half of the effects of the cyber-attack were spread over building distribution and the rest in industrial centers, particularly construction products; geographically, it was the countries of Western Europe that were most affected, with the Nordic countries, Germany and France being the most affected" (Saint-Gobain 2017).

"The NotPetya virus has contaminated computers via Ukrainian tax administration software to which companies must connect", says Claude Imauven, number 2 of the French group, interviewed by *L'Usine nouvelle* on February 9, 2018. In a few minutes, thousands of data were encrypted and impossible to recover. Computerized ordering and invoicing systems were blocked. The group's distribution networks, Point P and Lapeyre, had to return to pen and paper to write purchase orders and transmit them manually. It took four days of crisis management and 10 days for the business to fully resume.

According to Claude Imauven: "Learning to work in a degraded mode so as not to break continuity is the most central aspect of good risk management". This involves prioritizing the criticality of the various assets and taking preventive actions, identifying the various fallback solutions and mobilizing the various teams internally.

Phishing operations, intrusion tests … Today, the company regularly organizes full-scale tests to make employees aware of the various threats. In addition, Saint-Gobain now requires suppliers, who directly connect to the group's system, to be cybervirtuous "a *sine qua non* condition for us today", says the CEO.

At the same time, the company that was not covered against this type of risk at the time of the event undertook to insure itself against cyber-attacks.

Altran in France and Hydro in Norway

The technology consulting group Altran is forced to take a significant step back following the computer hacking of which it was the victim on January 23, 2019. This slow period can be very expensive for the group, especially in terms of image.

An Altran spokesman said that the company had been hit by a ransom, which is why it had to disconnect its computer network and all its applications "immediately" to prevent a spread. Altran is in contact with ANSSI, the French government information systems security agency:

> We have mobilized independent, internationally recognized technical and investigative experts, and the investigation we conducted with them has revealed no data theft or cases of propagation of the incident to our customers.

In particular, Altran carries out R&D (research and development) missions for major energy and transport groups, including Airbus. An attack on the company could therefore be aimed at gaining access to its customers' trade secrets.

In an interview with *Le Parisien*, Guillaume Poupard reports attacks "by State, private or terrorist actors who do not yet aim to destroy, but to set up and above all to study computer systems" in the three major sectors of energy, telecommunications and transport.

Le Monde informatique also indicates that, despite these recommendations, Altran has paid more than 300 bitcoins, or nearly 1 million euros, to receive the decryption key for the files. By the end of February, it had not been delivered, according to *L'Express*, which also quotes a financial analyst who estimates that the cost of the attack on Altran would already amount to 20 million euros.

It was this same ransom, LockerGoga, encrypting computer files and demanding money to make them available again, that partially paralyzed Norway's third largest hydropower producer and one of the world's largest aluminum producers, Norsk Hydro, on March 18, 2019. The attack was detected after abnormal activity on its servers around midnight. This cyber-attack intensified overnight, targeting the IT systems of most of the group's activities.

Isolated from the main grid, this being a good practice for critical installations, electricity production has not been affected. As a result of the attack, Hydro's website is inaccessible; Hydro communicates via its Facebook page.

Several extrusion plants, which transform aluminum ingots into metal parts for, for example, car manufacturers or the construction sector, have been closed, while its giant foundries in several countries such as Norway, Qatar and Brazil have switched to manual operation.

Quoting a message from the NSM, the Norwegian public broadcaster NRK reports on its website that pirates have demanded money from Norsk Hydro to stop their attack, which the group has not confirmed. We will return in detail to the crisis management implemented by Hydro in Chapter 6.

1.5. Examples of particularly exposed sectors of activity

1.5.1. *Cinema*

In November 2014, when Sony Pictures Entertainment employees turned on their computers, a skeleton image appeared, accompanied by a message of blackmail: the objective was to prevent the screening of the film *The Interview*. The pirates then broadcast four films that were to be released in the following months. The total loss for Sony amounted to more than 200 million dollars.

In addition, the personal data of Sony Pictures Entertainment employees were stolen by the hackers: name, address, social security number, driver's license number, passport number and/or other national identifier, bank account number, credit card information for business travel expenses, user name and passwords, remuneration and other employment related information, as well as medical data.

Since this incident, companies in the film industry have become extremely secure: external service providers, such as dubbing companies, receive encrypted files, file reading requires double or triple authentication and tasks are separated so that a very limited number of people have access to the entire film. Access to the editing, dubbing and recording rooms is very secure (access by badge or facial recognition). Information flows are constantly monitored. An anomaly can thus be quickly detected and the perpetrator identified and sanctioned.

1.5.2. *Banks*

Although no bank is immune to an incident, banks have strengthened their IT security over many years, particularly under the authority of the EBA (European Banking Authority) or the ACPR (French Prudential Supervision and Resolution Authority), which consider this risk as a main risk, in particular, because the information systems of banks, financial markets, customers and suppliers are interconnected.

All the banks' branches of activity are affected by digital transformation: their market activities, the operations of their individual (BtoC) or corporate (BtoB) customers, the setting up of financing and data processing (the volume of data processed by banks is huge) which is a crucial issue in terms of the development of services, new products and therefore of competitive advantage.

Cybersecurity threats are therefore a major concern for banks, which are required to strengthen their IT resources and control systems. Cyber-attacks on banks or banking networks in recent years have highlighted this risk and the potential impacts on banks' production or brand image.

Digital trust is critical for banks: how can customers trust a bank, if it does not ensure the functioning and security of means of payment, accessibility to quality information, if it is a victim of theft, if transfers are made without its knowledge and without its customers' knowledge and if it cannot protect its customers' data?

The ACPR (*Autorité de contrôle prudentiel et de résolution*) has identified three main risk themes: organization of the information system and its security, operation of the information system and information system security.

FINMA (Swiss Federal Financial Market Supervisory Authority) sees cyber-attacks as the main risk for banks (March 27, 2018). The head of FINMA points out that the effectiveness of a defense system is measured by its weakest link and invites the players in the sector to redouble their efforts in this area.

The latest statistics published by the Reporting and Analysis Centre for Information Assurance (MELANI) in Switzerland show that two-thirds of all cyber-attacks recorded concern the financial sector.

There are up to 100 attacks per day on e-banking solutions in Switzerland.

The cyber subject is at the top of the concerns of the managers of the big banks. The number of intrusions into financial institutions' computer systems has tripled over the past five years, according to a study conducted by Accenture and the American research institute Ponemon among 254 companies in seven countries (France, Italy, Japan, the United States, Germany, Italy and Australia).

Banks and other insurers are subjected to an average of 125 intrusions into their systems each year, compared with just 40 in 2012, compared with an average of 130 intrusions into companies outside the banking sector each year. It seems that these attacks have no financial impact (at least that is what the banks say).

But while these repeated security breaches result in few revenue losses, they disrupt service and threaten the integrity of customers' data and assets. They have an impact on the quality of service ("service suspensions are due to maintenance operations") and on the confidence that customers have in their banks. How to entrust your money to a bank that regularly offers online services that are inaccessible?

The spectrum of denial of service can be defined as follows: "Banks have become more resilient than other economic actors to traditional attacks such as malware, but they remain very sensitive to attacks that saturate their systems and cause denial of service", said Accenture. At the end of January 2018, ING, Rabobank and ABN Amro banks were attacked by "denial of service" (server sending massive simultaneous requests): these banks were unable to provide access to their online services in the Netherlands for several hours.

This more sophisticated type of threat is also the most expensive[3]. On average, according to the study, institutions spend $250,000 to deal with a denial of service compared to less than $100,000 for an attack using software that takes data hostage (ransom) or any other malicious software.

This encourages the inflation of cybercrime costs, which have increased considerably over the last three years in the financial sector. On average, according to the study, companies spent $18.28 million in 2017 to protect themselves, compared to $12.97 million in 2014. These amounts far exceed those committed by players in industry, aeronautics, technology and health: the report estimates that all sectors of activity commit $11.7 million per year to protect themselves.

With the rise of mobile banking and new technologies, the threat promises to increase.

As Laurent Mignon, current CEO of the BPCE group, stated on February 16, 2018, in *Les Échos* – he was then CEO of Natixis – "the only systemic risk for the banking system is cyber-risk", while adding: "The financial system is more aware of this risk than other industries. The regulator has been ensuring that it has been taken into account for many years".

---

3 Source: https://www.lesechos.fr/2018/03/le-risque-cyber-est-de-plus-en-plus-menacant-dans-la-finance-987502.

In May 2019, Sabine Lautenschläger, member of the Executive Board of the European Central Bank (ECB), reported that between July 2017 and September 2018, 66 major IT security incidents were reported to the ECB. "I am afraid that the incident report we have at our disposal will not provide an overview of the situation", she added.

As a reminder, the first major cyber-attack targeting a European banking institution occurred in 2016: the accounts of 40,000 customers of Tesco Bank, a subsidiary of the British supermarket chain, had been hacked, 20,000 of whom were reportedly fraudulently withdrawn. In January 2017, a denial of service attack targeted several major British banks and made Lloyds Bank's online services unavailable for two days.

In June 2019, for the first time, a simulation of a cross-border cyber-attack in finance is being organized by G7 members, as announced by the French authorities. Coordinated by the Banque de France, this exercise must involve 24 financial authorities (central banks, supervisors, ministries of finance, market authorities) from seven countries. Representatives of the private sector in France, Italy, Germany and Japan will also be involved:

> Beyond that, according to François Villeroy de Galhau, it is also necessary to work on a 'common categorization' of cyber incidents and to provide more information to measure the intensity and sophistication of threats and their evolution.[4]

"It is time for financial institutions to take radical measures to strengthen their fight against cyber-attacks. It is expensive and complex, but absolutely necessary", said Bruno Lemaire, the French Finance Minister, in May 2019.

1.5.3. *Health*

The health sector, and, in particular, hospitals, is one of the sectors that is subject to repeated attacks and in which security investments are insufficient, although cybersecurity is considered a major issue by health equipment suppliers.

---

4 Source: https://www.lesechos.fr/finance-marches/banque-insurance/cybersecurity-in-finance-france-military-for-a-convergence-of-regulations-1018036.

Indeed, medical records also include information relating to mutual insurance or insurance contracts, and billing information, which allows us to identity theft and lucrative fraud.

Hospitals are often poorly protected: lack of resources, lack of budget, administrative burdens, governance difficulties (balance of power between the medical profession and functional teams) and furthermore cannot afford to stop their activities, for obvious reasons of risk to patients. They are therefore interesting targets for cybercriminals.

Cybersecurity Ventures predicts that computer attacks through ransom (malware that takes personal data hostage: it encrypts personal data and then asks its owner to send money in exchange for the key to decrypt it) will increase fivefold between 2018 and 2021.

In the United States, the U.S. Food and Drug Administration (FDA) warned on March 21, 2019, that some of Medtronic's connected medical devices, including implantable cardiac defibrillators, had cybersecurity vulnerabilities.

"Companies must take steps to monitor and assess cyber security vulnerability risks, and be proactive in disclosing them", it insists.

It recalls that "any medical device connected to a communication network" may have security breaches, although these devices and software "may also offer a safer, more convenient and faster delivery of care".

By October 2018, Medtronic had to disable Internet updates for some 34,000 CareLink programming devices for healthcare professionals worldwide to access existing pacemakers, as it found the system vulnerable to cyber-attacks.

1.5.4. *Tourism and business hotels*

The tourism and business hotel sector has been attacked many times in recent years: the theft of names, postal addresses and emails, the company name and telephone number of Radisson Rewards program members were disclosed in October 2018. They were notified so that they could detect any suspicious activity, and Radisson recommended that they not respond to any requests from the Rewards program regarding their personal information, including usernames and passwords.

In June 2018, the hotel reservation site Fastbooking, a subsidiary of AccorHotels, was hacked, and the names, email addresses and credit card numbers of hundreds of hotels' customers were hacked (reservations of May and June 2017).

In March 2018, Orbitz, a subsidiary of Expedia, became aware of a major piracy that targeted it between January 2016 and December 2017. For nearly 24 months, a security breach was therefore present on the site specialized in booking flights, as well as online travel.

In 2016, Hyatt Hotels Corporation reported a theft of credit card data from 250 hotels. In the same year, Hilton, Mandarin Oriental, Trump Hotels and Starwood Hotels & Resorts Worldwide were the target of computer attacks.

The hacking of personal data held by hotel chains is a problem for people who can then be victims of fraud and identity theft; sometimes, it is also confidential data concerning the movement of personalities.

1.5.5. *Critical national infrastructure*

1.5.5.1. *Military Programming Act*

IT problems that could be attributed to critical national infrastructure could have systemic consequences on the functioning of the country and beyond: approximately in France, 200 entities are considered as critical national infrastructure in the transport, energy, finance, health and telecommunications sectors. These companies are particularly supervised by the State and are subject to regulatory obligations: LPM, or Military Programming Law, adopted in 2013, decree published in 2015 and European NIS directive, adopted in 2016.

ANSSI's mission is to support operators of vital importance in securing their sensitive information systems. This system has made it possible to identify private and public critical national infrastructure that operate or use facilities considered essential for the nation's survival.

The 2013 LPM imposes a number of rules relating to the cybersecurity of critical national infrastructure and defines their responsibilities and obligations in terms of protecting their critical information systems.

It thus requires critical national infrastructure to have their VISs (vital information systems) audited by qualified organizations (SSI audit providers) and to implement security measures for information systems and qualified detection systems. Critical national infrastructure must also immediately report ISS incidents that significantly affect their ISS.

The various cybersecurity rules of the critical national infrastructure concern the control of information systems (mapping and maintaining security conditions), the management of security incidents (logs of key events and analysis of these logs, implementation of sensors to detect anomalies, implementation of an incident management organization, processing of alerts, incident processing, crisis management) and system protection (identification, authentication, access management, administrator account management, information system partitioning, flow management, remote access, update management, procedures for installing new equipment or implementing new services).

1.5.5.2. *Issues for officers and directors*

Since compliance is a major point of vigilance for the board of directors, the directors of qualified critical national infrastructure companies will be required to understand the risks and ensure compliance with these rules.

Directors of companies that are not critical to national infrastructure can also use these rules as a model to improve the cybersecurity maturity of their companies.

1.6. Responsibilities of officers and directors

All sectors are concerned, and the sustainability of the company is at stake, because attacks can be serious, the value of the company can be brutally impacted, and the shareholders of a listed company or a large family business, as well as stakeholders, can therefore legitimately question whether the board of directors and shareholders have been concerned about this issue and have taken the necessary measures.

Are they competent? Did they ask the right questions? What information do they receive?

– Who is in charge of IT security? Even if the position does not exist, someone must have the responsibility of information systems security. To whom is it attached? What is the scope of their responsibilities?

– When was the last time I heard about cybersecurity? Putting the topic on the Comex agenda is simple and essential. First of all informative, this subject raises the competence of top management, which will have a more relevant and involved approach. A quarterly review, even if it is fast, is already a good pace. Your CISO can also present cases of cyber-attacks relayed by the press by showing how your company is concerned or would have reacted.

– When did I tell the whole company about cybersecurity? When was the last time you sent a message to raise awareness among your teams? Are they aware of the main risks? A regular information and awareness campaign must be set up.

– How intense are the attacks on my company? All companies are under attack on their information systems. Are you aware of the volume and frequency of those that affect your business? Do you know if your teams have already successfully prevented a major attack?

– Am I personally exposed? At the heart of your company's strategy, you are a prime target, and your media presence focuses the interest of hackers, who measure your maturity and appetite for cybersecurity. The first way to protect yourself is therefore to start by applying the recommended rules and instructions, which are themselves respected by your employees. They will be all the more motivated by your exemplarity.

Box 1.1. *The five questions to ask yourself regularly*

Corporate Governance and Digital Responsibility

2.1. Corporate governance and stakeholders

As Hervé Guillou stated in October 2016 at a conference:

> The subject of cybersecurity is both an economic development issue for companies and a national security and resilience issue: an economic issue because cybersecurity is a catalyst for the digital transformation of the company, at the heart of the protection of its industrial and intellectual heritage and therefore of its value[1].

Hervé Guillou adds the following information:

> Needless to say, the subject of cybersecurity must be a major concern for business leaders and boards of directors. It directly concerns the company's image, its sustainability, its strategic and commercial positioning and is therefore strictly in the company's corporate interest.

The main objective of good governance is to ensure that shareholders and all stakeholders have confidence in the sustainability of the company, some because they invest in a company, others because they work for it as an

---

1 Conference organized by HEC Gouvernance with Alain Juillet, Guillaume Poupard and Alain Bouillé (CESIN) in October 2016.

employee or subcontractor, or because it is a critical partner, banks involved in the credits set up, tax authorities or social organizations.

Governance is the system that organizes the relationships and powers between shareholders, the board of directors and managers, to ensure the proper management of the company, the creation of value, limit risks, guide strategic decisions, supervise the proper execution of the strategy and control the company's performance to ensure the best interests of shareholders, while contributing to the safeguarding of the interests of all stakeholders.

The board of directors has a major role: it represents shareholders, guides strategy, appoints and controls management. The role of directors has increased, due to the greater complexity of the economy, linked in particular to international competition, a strengthened international regulatory environment, and the emergence of new technologies that are transforming business models and the organization of the company and its ecosystem. The emergence of new risks as a result of all these phenomena increases the responsibilities of the boards of directors, whose skills must evolve, as well as the areas of vigilance.

The digital transformation of the economy has consequences on the information available to shareholders, the board of directors and all stakeholders. The new challenges for the company's governance bodies are numerous: e-reputation, price volatility, dematerialization of operations, protection of board information, disintermediation and emergence of new players, which can have significant impacts on the company's valuation.

2.2. The shareholders

Beyond the strategic risks associated with the entry of new competitors, the digital transformation of companies, the connections of its information systems with its customers, suppliers, banks and administrations increase IT risks, the risks of fraud and vulnerabilities to attacks, which can lead to either operational problems or data leaks.

2.2.1. *Valuation of the company*

The valuation of the company depends on the quality of its strategy and execution. The digital strategy in all its dimensions is essential: digital transformation is not an end in itself, but a means to access new markets, develop new products and services, as well as to improve sales, production and management processes.

In addition, the company's resilience, i.e. its ability to restart its information, production or sales systems, to protect them, to anticipate crises, to set up solutions to detect and respond to incidents and finally its ability to take the right corrective measures following the attack, is essential for shareholders and value creation.

According to a study conducted by PwC France (PricewaterhouseCoopers) in 2018 on around 30 incidents, more than half of the companies suffered a stock market loss of between 10% and 20% more than a year after the incident, and consequently a loss of market confidence. For about 20% of companies, the price fell by 6% in the first 10 days, but the price recovered in the following 6–12 months, thanks to good crisis management, the implementation of cybersecurity measures and investments, as well as communication on these measures that helped to restore market confidence.

Cyber-attacks exert an impact on the stock price if they are the result of proven negligence, as in the case of Equifax in the United States (the price dropped by 40%; the administration's recommendations regarding software updates were not followed by Equifax) or Talk Talk in the United Kingdom (the price dropped by 30% because the sensitive data was not encrypted), but have no lasting impact on the share price, if measures are taken in terms of management (general management, IT and IT security department, security policies, training, strengthening IT and security budgets) and if customer confidence has not been lost.

The market's response will therefore depend on the vigilance of the board of directors and managers, before and after, on its skills and responsiveness, as well as on its awareness of digital issues, the feedback that will have been organized by the board of directors and the procedures put in place, particularly regarding risk mapping.

The cyber avoiders sitting on the board of directors are not an asset for shareholders, regardless of the risk area, and in particular for all cybersecurity and data protection issues.

Conversely, even if no company is immune to attack, computer crashes and data leaks, anticipating, being vigilant and implementing a cybersecurity system will be an asset to the company's reputation and the trust of all stakeholders.

2.2.2. *Cyber rating agencies*

Cyber rating agencies have been developed in the United States and are based in Europe. Their objective is to highlight facts and events related to the cybersecurity of organizations' assets and to compare them with the best cybersecurity standards and practices.

There is also a greater willingness on the part of shareholders, gathered in groups of institutional investors, investment funds or activist shareholders, to engage in corporate governance. Activist shareholders will want to know if the companies in which they have invested are well secured. Indeed, cybersecurity will increasingly become a topic for shareholders (risk of loss of value).

As a result of this significant risk of loss of value, shareholders will increasingly seek to know what measures companies have in place, require information on risks and remediation measures, and will be vigilant about compliance with new regulations and about the confidence that customers can place in a company's ability to protect data, and in particular its customers' data. This trust will depend on the company's transparency on its methods of collecting and protecting the data it holds, and in particular those of its customers.

After Standard & Poor's drew attention to cyber-risks, particularly in the banking sector, it is now Moody's turn to include cybersecurity among the criteria for evaluating companies. The risk involved is such that investors must be informed of the level of protection against cyber-attacks.

"We expect companies to set up cybersecurity steering bodies", warns Moody at the end of November 2015. IT security managers are no longer the only ones to sound the alarm.

2.2.3. *Insider trading*

Increased vigilance is needed regarding the risks of insider trading following a cyber incident. The Equifax example is a famous example not to be followed. In September 2017, Equifax, the US credit agency, was the victim of a major data leak: 143 million victims. This data leak, discovered between mid-May and July, was announced to the market in early September. As a result of this announcement, the value of Equifax decreased by 40%.

The SEC (Securities and Exchange Commission), the US stock exchange police, charged several Equifax executives with selling their shares before the news of the hacking of personal data (names, social security numbers, birth dates, etc.) was made public.

The piracy allegedly cost the company more than 150 million and had significant impacts in terms of reputation and loss of customers, the investigation having revealed in particular negligence on the part of managers regarding the cybersecurity system.

Another case that made headlines in the United States at the end of 2017 was the sale by Intel's CEO of part of his shares for $39 million ($25 million capital gain), before the disclosure of critical vulnerabilities in Intel processors, and several months after he discovered these vulnerabilities.

In addition, the SEC considers cybersecurity to be a vital issue for all organizations. It requires listed companies to inform the markets by publishing a form detailing the cyber-attacks they have been subjected to, as these events may jeopardize a company's future.

The rules established by the SEC prohibit managers of listed companies from selling their shares when they become aware of information that could affect the share price.

It is therefore recommended that employees holding shares or stock options be informed of the rules governing the sale of these shares, depending on the time of year and the information they may hold on events that may have an impact on the share price.

2.2.4. *Activist shareholders*

The amounts managed by so-called "activist" investment funds increased from $27 billion to $163 billion between 2007 and 2017. One of the characteristics of these activist funds is to interfere in the management of listed companies, with a strategic vision in the short or long term.

Some recent European examples include TCI (The Children's Investment Fund), which challenged Safran's takeover of Zodiac, which was considered "overpaid" and "non-rational" and which also "encouraged" Airbus to sell its shares in Dassault. Third Point called for a major reorientation of Nestlé's strategy and the sale of its stake in L'Oréal. Cevian Capital, an activist fund of Swedish origin, acquired a stake in Rexel, modified its executive committee and launched an asset disposal program. Cevian Capital is also leading ABB (the Swiss leader in advanced technologies, a world leader in digital industries with four leading business sectors in their respective fields: electrification, industrial automation, mobility and robotics) to sell Power Grids, representing one-third of its activities.

The arrival of an activist fund in the capital is never a trivial event for a listed company. Their interventions in the media aim to denounce the flaws they intend to correct, in order to accelerate the creation of value (often in the short term) and its sharing with shareholders.

From a strategic point of view, digital transformation and the speed with which companies adapt to new market access, competition, product and service offerings and production capacity are the best means of avoiding activist funds.

From the point of view of the company's reputation and the trust of customers and stakeholders, securing information systems and data protection are also the best ways to avoid impairment, the inflow of activist funds into the capital and the brutal restructuring of the company.

For administrators, it is following a cybersecurity incident and a drop in share prices that the real problems begin: shareholders lawsuits, capital restructuring and equity investments by activist shareholders, who benefit from the decline in the share price.

The company distracted by the crisis management, the functioning of IT resources, communication with customers and the media, disputes and investigations on the responsibilities involved, will at the same time be disrupted by shareholders who will publicly call for the resignation of the main directors.

Resignations of senior executives and/or shareholder disputes have already affected Target, Wyndham Worldwide, TJX and Heartland Payment Systems. Others will follow.

2.2.5. *The stock exchange authorities*

The SEC, the US stock exchange authority, is very attentive to the impacts of cybercrime on companies. It published a Cyber-Related Frauds Perpetrated Against Public Companies report in October 2018, following a survey of nine listed companies that have been victims of cyberfraud, ranging from $1 million to $45 million (payments to foreign accounts) through fake emails from executives or suppliers.

Many of these frauds were not sophisticated. As is often the case in cyber-attacks, criminals have relied on technology, as well as on procedural flaws and human vulnerabilities, making the control environment ineffective.

Procedures are sometimes correct, but staff are not trained and are not aware of the risks associated with cybercrime, such as identity theft, allowed by new technologies.

Given the highly malicious nature of cybercrime, the SEC will continue to play a leading role in regulating the cyber practices of American companies.

2.2.6. *The annual report*

The annual report is a means for shareholders to learn about the company's governance, strategy, accounts, risks and programs to address these risks, as well as the transfer of these risks to insurance.

The *Autorité des marchés financiers* (AMF) requires listed companies to publish certain information. At the general meeting, only the annual financial report is required: this document includes the annual corporate and consolidated financial statements, a management report, as well as a report from the statutory auditors.

The registration document provides more complete information about the company. More voluminous than the annual report, it includes, for example, a description of market activities, products and services, a group organization chart, an analysis of its financial situation, its main shareholders, its corporate and consolidated financial statements and their appendices.

These are very rich and include accounting rules and methods, as well as many elements on the company's financial situation, its tangible and intangible fixed assets, its holdings in partner companies, etc. The profitability by sector or geographical area is also presented.

It is therefore an excellent source of information, integrating information on risks (including risks related to information systems) and measures put in place. The famous 2017 attacks (Notpetya and Wannacry) were the starting point for these communications for most CAC 40 companies in France.

Strangely enough, there are still a few large companies that do not mention the subject, as if cyber-risks did not exist. It is true that companies do not want to spread their vulnerabilities in the public arena.

Nevertheless, it is important that shareholders are informed of the committees in charge and that they know whether these issues have been placed on the agenda of the board of directors or its committees, whether independent experts have been appointed to audit the organization, processes, systems and security policies.

Finally, the annual report describes the composition of the board of directors, the career path of each director, their skills, the composition of the committees and the work carried out during the year.

It is important to be concerned about a company that discusses these topics very briefly, does not have the appropriate skills on its board of directors and whose specialized committees (audit/risks) have not discussed the subject at least twice a year. Legal risks are increasing, as we will see in detail in Chapter 3.

2.3. The board of directors

2.3.1. *The facts*

Seventy-five percent of companies are not prepared for such a situation and are not sufficiently suspicious. A 2016 study by Spencer Stuart shows that the second threat to the 4,000 administrators surveyed are cybersecurity risks (after overregulation).

Spencer Stuart's survey of cybersecurity on boards of directors in the United States in 2017 reveals the following facts:

– most boards (69%) assign the responsibility for the oversight of cybersecurity to a committee of the board, while 26% say that the board as a whole manages cybersecurity risks;

– 57% of respondents stated that the audit committee monitors cybersecurity. In other boards, cybersecurity risk is overseen by the risk committee (7%), technology committee (4%) or nominating and governance committee (2%);

– 64% of respondents reported that the board of directors or a committee had developed a crisis management plan for cyber-infringement in the past year.

2.3.2. *The four missions of the board of directors*

The directors, meeting within the board of directors, participate in the management of the company, in a collegial manner, by determining its orientations and policies (the implementation of which is ensured by the general management) and by controlling its operation.

Directors must "watch over" and thus guarantee stakeholders that the company is managed with a view to its sustainability and sustainable performance. The board of directors is an essential factor of trust.

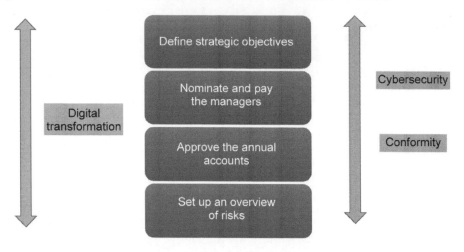

Figure 2.1. *The four missions of the board of directors (source: Starboard Advisory)*

The development of information technologies concerns the board of directors in all its dimensions:

– the definition of strategic objectives: market access, business model, marketing via digital channels, design of new products, production, distribution and management;

– the appointment of managers: consider the skills needed to achieve objectives, how to change the company's culture and support change through training;

– the closing of the accounts requires that the quality of the information and therefore of the information systems be ensured;

– the risk landscape will take into account cyber-risks and their potential impacts on financial performance, non-compliance risks and reputational risks, particularly following a data leak (personal, intellectual property, strategic data).

2.3.3. *Civil and criminal liability*

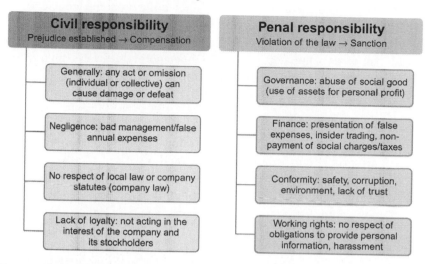

Figure 2.2. *Civil and criminal liability of executives (source: Starboard Advisory)*

A major disaster can impact the company's financial health and its own assets and make managers liable before the courts.

The manager's civil liability is engaged if, through a fault on his/her part – such as the lack of backup – the company suffers a loss of data that is very harmful to him/her. Civil liability is also incurred in the event of a proven lack of organizational measures or protection of the company's information system.

According to article 34, French law no. 2004-801 of August 6, 2004, relating to data processing, files and freedoms:

> The controller is required to take all necessary precautions, having regard to the nature of the data and the risks presented by the processing, to preserve the security of the data and, in particular, to prevent them from being distorted, damaged or accessed by unauthorized third parties.

Failure to comply with these data security obligations may also result in severe financial penalties imposed by the CNIL: on April 17, 2019, Optical Center was fined 200,000 euros.

Managers must therefore implement technical and organizational measures to protect the personal data they collect in the course of their activities against unauthorized, accidental or unlawful destruction, loss, alteration, dissemination or access: blocking intrusion and virus attempts (firewall, antivirus), updates, password management, access management, encryption, anonymization, pseudonymization, securing physical IT infrastructures (premises security).

In addition, managers must take legal measures: charters for the use of IT tools and networks (user and administrator charters), security clearance policies and procedures, data retention and archiving policies, use of applications, connection to websites, access by suppliers or subcontractors, mobility, use of personal tools, access to the Internet for personal reasons using company equipment and an incident management policy.

It is also recommended to set up delegations of authority between the manager and the CIO (Chief Information Officer)/CISO (Chief Information Security Officer), ensuring, as with any delegation of authority, that these managers have the technical skills, authority and means to exercise their responsibilities and that the delegation is express, limited and precise.

Let us recall article 226-17 of the French Criminal Code: "Any person responsible for the computer processing of personal data must adopt physical (security of premises) and logical (security of information systems) measures adapted to the nature of the data and the risks presented by the processing".

Failure to comply with this safety obligation is heavily sanctioned by French article 226-17: up to five years' imprisonment and a fine of 300,000 euros.

2.3.4. *The board of directors and cybersecurity*

Why does the board of directors have to take over cyber-risks? Mainly for financial, legal and reputational reasons. The three priorities are resilience, ethics and compliance. The stakes associated with cyber-attacks can be high, and board members should not wait until an attack occurs to assess the risks to which their company is exposed.

The *Institut Montaigne* (created by Claude Bébéar, chaired by Henri de Castries) brings together business executives, senior civil servants, academics and representatives of civil society. It is a space for reflection, free and independent of any political and economic constraints.

According to a report published in October 2018 by the Institute, based on a Wavestone study, only 25% of CAC 40 groups directly address cybersecurity issues at the executive committee level. Only 12% of CAC 40 companies report that they have launched a cybersecurity program. Only 58% of CAC 40 companies mentioned the GDPR in their registration documents in 2017.

The institute underlines the lack of awareness among management teams and the lack of integration of cybersecurity into corporate strategy. It proposes to encourage the preparation of a confidential (non-public) report on cyber-risks available to directors and to partially integrate these risks and countermeasures into the annual report.

According to an Opinion Way study, 54% of business leaders believe that cybersecurity is a matter for IT management and only 24% for senior management. However, this is a strategic issue for the board of directors and not an operational one, as some directors claim.

2.3.4.1. *Taking charge of the company's digital destiny*

Effective cybersecurity begins with risk awareness on the part of board members and senior executives who must recognize that the company can be attacked at any time. Risk mapping is therefore the starting point.

Cyber-risk is a risk that you will have to get used to living with. Ensure that mechanisms are in place to enable the company to be more resilient (in particular to guarantee the accessibility of the system, its proper functioning, the confidentiality of information and its integrity). Directors and officers are responsible for controlling this risk.

The board of directors has, among other things, a legal obligation to monitor the effectiveness of the company's risk management system. With regard to cyber-risks, it is therefore necessary to ensure that operational managers are aware of the risks and new regulations, and if the size of the company allows it, provide the company with a global risk management system.

Finally, the risk analysis may lead to a transfer of risks to insurance. Although cyber-risks are complex and difficult to quantify, particularly because of the lack of historical loss data and the wide variety of incidents that can occur, insurance companies are positioning themselves in this market and have an analytical grid that allows the company to better understand its level of risk and protection.

Ratings, as discussed in section 2.2.2, are a tool and a point of vigilance for boards of directors, and in particular audit committees. They allow a quick audit to be carried out and the progress of improvements to be monitored. It would be better to anticipate these ratings before they become public.

2.3.4.2. *Reinventing the board of directors?*

Directors are not IT experts and are not intended to be. Beyond the digital strategy and the transformation of the business model, it is nevertheless necessary to understand the laws, threats, risks, consequences, roles and responsibilities, and methods to protect the company.

The difficulty for the board of directors and managers stems in particular from a lack of a common vocabulary on cybersecurity issues that is understandable by all, as well as objective data to assess, manage, compare and decide on cyber performance.

First of all, it is a question of improving communication between the IT department and the rest of the company: one in four IT decision makers do not inform their management in the event of cyber-attacks.

Corporate boards of directors can set up a digital committee, as Schneider Electric did in 2017, or a security committee, as the Richemont group in Switzerland has done, capable of managing and controlling cyber-risks and crisis management, and offer more digital training to directors:

– Schneider Electric's digital committee is dedicated to digital strategy and performance. It holds at least three meetings per year, including the joint review of cybersecurity risks with the audit and risk committee. It prepares the Board's work by examining seven subjects in greater depth: development and growth of the digital business, improvement and transformation of the digital experience of the group's customers and partners, improvement of

Schneider Electric's operational efficiency through the effective use of training technologies and digital automation capabilities, cyber-risk assessment and improvement of the Group's position in cybersecurity (jointly with the audit committee), assessment of the contribution of possible M&A transactions to the Group's digital strategy, monitoring and analysis of the digital environment (competitors and processors, threats and opportunities), and verification that the company has the appropriate human resources for digital transformation;

– the Richemont group (luxury industry in Switzerland) has created a Strategic Security Committee (SSC), which meets four times a year. Its responsibility is to advise the board of directors on all aspects of security policies; its objective is to protect the company's assets, including confidential information and intellectual property, as well as its operations against intrusive actions. The committee also supervises property and persons.

2.3.5. *The board of directors and data protection*

It is no secret that we entered the era of Big Data, which consists of capturing, analyzing, sharing and storing digital data. Big Data is powered by e-commerce, and services will be powered by the Internet of Things, autonomous cars or drones in the future.

More and more companies are experiencing cyber-attacks and data leaks, such as Yahoo!, Equifax, Facebook or British Airways. These two observations raise the problem of digital trust and therefore that of digital responsibility.

The risks are high enough for investors, and in particular responsible investment, to get involved. NEI Investments, Canada's leading provider of responsible investment solutions, owned Facebook securities in three of its funds.

At Facebook's general shareholders' meeting in 2018, NEI Investments voted against all members of the board of directors, considering that they had failed to protect their users' data.

The GDPR (General Data Protection Regulation) could be expensive, very expensive for Web giants and other actors. Complaints have been filed against Google and Facebook. In total, $8.8 billion is being claimed from the two American companies.

Concerning the company's compliance with the GDPR, there are two main topics:

– what do companies do with the data collected; have they received user consent and for which services have they received consent?

– how are data and information systems protected?

In conclusion, the board of directors shall:

– acquire the skills and committees adapted to its sector of activity, strategy and risks;

– check that the cyber-risk is on the CEO's agenda (it starts with the CEO!);

– inform itself (be diligent) and challenge the managers;

– regularly audit the systems (organization, processes, tools and teams), with the help of trusted and long-term service providers;

– include cyber information in the annual report.

2.3.6. *The statutory auditors*

The main mission of the statutory auditors is to certify the regularity and sincerity of the accounts. It is permanent and includes obligations toward the partners. Through their knowledge of companies' procedures and systems, the auditor has a real role to play with them, in particular to measure the company's exposure and maturity to cyber-risks, assess the financial impacts (ransoms, fraud against the president, fraud against "false RIBs", fines) and write a report for the attention of managers.

In particular, their role is to alert management so that the company can modify the rules and improve the application of security rules when it has identified breaches of IT security standards that may damage the company's financial assets.

If necessary, the external auditors/internal auditors may recommend to the CFO or audit committee an audit of the company's information systems and processes by an external expert.

The *Compagnie nationale des commissaires aux comptes* (CNCC) has developed the CyberAUDIT© tool, which measures the company's exposure and maturity to cyber-risks, assesses the financial impacts and prepares a report for managers.

The auditors can be considered as partners of the board of directors, both for the certification of the accounts and also for the company's cyber performance: its processes, its organization and its information systems.

2.3.7. *The numerical responsibility of the board of directors*

Beyond cybersecurity and data protection issues, the board of directors must reconcile its social and environmental responsibility with its digital responsibility.

Indeed, digital transformation, automation and robotization have consequences:

– societal: employment (elimination of certain jobs, as well as relocation of certain industries), skills, employability of personnel, organization of the company, working methods, labor legislation (teleworking, disappearance of borders between the workplace and the home, etc.), training;

– environmental: depletion of non-renewable resources, energy costs (IT is a major consumer of electricity, and energy costs are increasing in line with the digital transformations of society as a whole), recycling of equipment.

This increase in energy consumption linked to digital technology can be offset by remote working (videoconferencing, teleworking, working in coworking centers) to limit the cost of travel, dematerialization of documents, eco-design of products and software, staff awareness of eco-responsible behavior, purchases of equipment that uses less energy, better building management, adaptation and optimization of behavior, and therefore a better ecological and energy transition.

Beyond the security and sustainability of the company, it will therefore be the responsibility of the board of directors, and the digital committee if it is formed, to ensure the social and environmental impacts of the digital strategy.

2.4. Customers and suppliers

Customer satisfaction in a BtoC (Business to Consumer) activity, such as online sales or online banking, is closely linked to the quality of the cybersecurity and data protection measures implemented by their product or service providers.

The trust that customers place in their suppliers is not only linked to the quality of the products or services purchased but also to the quality and security of the website, the means of payment, the level of protection of the data collected and stored by the supplier in the course of these transactions, as well as the respect of consents given or refused when connecting to the website.

These cybersecurity and customer data protection efforts have a cost, as well as an essential competitive advantage.

According to a 2018 Capgemini Digital Transformation Institute study of 6,000 consumers, cybersecurity and data protection are the third most important criterion when choosing an online supplier, after product or service quality and availability, and before selling price and price discounts, brand reputation and the guarantee that the product will be replaced or refunded if it is defective or damaged.

Among the customer requests, the most frequent ones are the following:

– encryption of saved data;

– password request;

– clarity of the data privacy policy;

– possibility of controlling the stored data and the duration of the archiving of this data;

– use of antivirus software;

– use of encryption tools on websites and applications;

– double authentication, with a mobile phone or a fingerprint.

This study also shows that:

– consumers have a perception of cybersecurity and data protection efforts that is lower than the level that their suppliers say or believe they have reached;

– consumers would buy more online if they had more guarantees.

The main reasons for this discrepancy are:

– failures in connected objects, poor segregation of duties, old infrastructure, inadequate security tools, vulnerable payment systems, lack of data encryption and employee errors;

– a lack of communication from suppliers on the efforts undertaken;

– a lack of transparency on data theft (40% of online retailers had leaks of personal and confidential data between 2015 and 2017). Indeed, 31% of suppliers (retailers) did not notify their customers before they were informed by the press. The GDPR regulation should improve this transparency, since companies have 72 hours to inform the authorities (CNIL, *Commission nationale de l'informatique et des libertés* in France, for example, and ICO, Information Commissioner, in the UK) and to inform their customers, in case of high risk (theft of credit cards, for example).

The conclusion of this study focuses on recommendations to gain the trust of their customers and to obtain a better turnover with each of them:

– understand their expectations, be at the forefront of cybersecurity devices and be ahead of hackers; focus efforts on protecting the data collected;

– monitor and audit information systems and transactions on a daily basis to detect anomalies;

– train employees regularly and systematically train new employees (high staff turnover in e-commerce activities);

– strengthen security measures: antivirus (firewalls) and authentication systems (with a sufficient password length).

Following a data leak, e-commerce companies generally focus on two main actions: implementing solutions to protect themselves from APTs (Advanced Persistent Threats) and setting up a SOC (Surveillance Operation Center) to detect and prevent fraud. However, the following actions are not considered priorities: data costing, systems and network redesign, recruitment of experts and judicial investigation.

2.5. Operational management

2.5.1. *The impacts of digital transformation*

The board of directors must ask itself the question of the operational management's digital skills, which is in charge of defining the strategy and proposing it to the board of directors: the search for the right balance between the digital revolution and the skills of the general management can lead to strengthening the Management Board, rebalancing it and training it in new technologies.

Indeed, these offer new opportunities, as well as have a strong influence on working methods, the organization and culture of the company, hierarchical links and relations with the outside world. Digital transformations also present significant risks: lack of proximity, loss of meaning, internationalization, displacement of power, changes in the value chain, the emergence of new professions and the disappearance of traditional ones.

Digital transformation also requires an adaptation of remuneration methods: multi-channel changes the proportion of turnover coming from physical sites and individual commercial approaches. The tools allow information sharing and productivity gains, production methods, cost and deadline improvements and quality controls are based on the introduction of information systems and numerical controls.

This transformation requires skills, training, organizational change and investment.

It is not without risks: matrix organizations, reduction in intermediate management, acceleration and short-term management, multiplication of coordination meetings and, of course, technological challenges, risks of cyber-attacks, amount of investments, loss of proximity with customers, decrease in quality and positioning in the value chain.

2.5.2. *The digital strategy*

Implementing governance and digital strategy in the company to meet security challenges is a responsibility of managers: data, product and information system security (general IT, production, products, sales, support functions), data identification and critical systems.

It is also a responsibility of the board of directors, which must examine the new opportunities offered by digital technologies and review the objectives to ensure the company's sustainability. It must then choose the best strategy to achieve these objectives, monitor its execution and analyze the risks to control them.

The use of new digital technologies is not an end in itself, but a means to reach new customers and markets, to offer new products and services, and even to improve the company's performance, gain efficiency and optimize the business model (selling prices, cost prices, investments, etc.).

Even if it is not an end in itself, the board of directors cannot ignore the examination of objectives and strategy with a digital prism, both from an opportunity and a risk point of view. This review will of course be different for each sector of activity and each type of company.

An in-depth analysis of customers and the evolution of their habits and requirements, competitors, new players and innovations in their sector of activity, as well as possible transformations of the company's processes, will be essential for directors. The results of this monitoring and the analyses of this information should be shared by the board of directors.

Digital technology offers new commercial channels and can make it possible to switch from a BtoB model to a BtoC model, to internationalize, to communicate widely and quickly (websites, social networks) to strengthen one's brand and improve competitiveness by reducing costs (production, inventory management, information exchanges with suppliers and subcontractors, quality improvement).

The quality of the data collected and the analysis of this data will be essential to develop commercial offers, customer relations and payment methods.

On the other hand, it can constitute a major strategic risk if competitors go faster and take market share, if the execution (commercial or production side) is not of good quality or if the dependence on distribution platforms is too high (the dereferencing of the platform can, in this case, be fatal to the company) and if the company is the victim of cyber-attacks or false information on the Internet.

The digital technology will not be systematically retained by the boards of directors, who may prefer to maintain a significant amount of proximity to customers, while offering them the possibility of using digital tools, if they so wish. Complexity is the enemy of security.

2.5.2.1. *Several possible and complementary answers*

Compromises between security and agility

A Censuswide study shows that 94% of CIOs and CISOs make compromises with security to avoid affecting the company's business.

We all make compromises with our safety or with the safety of the company and risk taking. IT security is no exception to this reality. But, as with the physical security of a home, there are rules from which we cannot deviate, depending on where we live. Investing in a digicode and publishing the code on Facebook, or installing an intercom and letting everyone in without asking their name, would make no sense.

Similarly, the most sophisticated surveillance tools, antivirus programs and firewalls are not useful if access management is not rigorously administered (remove temporary access given to external service providers, fixed-term employees, temporary workers, interns), if passwords are not updated regularly, if the information is not classified with access management in accordance with the company's security policies and if the exchange of confidential information (e.g. board of directors' information) is not strictly reserved for authorized persons, with secure storage and appropriate encryption.

Sellers of ultra-secure solutions say it immediately when they present their miracle solution: the management of the tool, access, flows, the decision to encrypt or not is not their responsibility. It is therefore not enough to buy tools; it is also necessary to analyze the need, check the integration into the existing IT environment, train users in the functionalities of the tool, its objectives and points of vigilance and then appoint an administrator, who can define the rules, organization and processes, who is authorized to modify, update, add, delete a document.

Updates are a good example of a source of compromise: according to the same study, 81% of respondents indicate that they have already refrained from deploying a "significant" update and 52% from doing so several times, in order not to affect the company's operations and avoid downtime, to avoid affecting legacy systems, or as a result of internal pressures from other company departments, for which the company's resilience is not a priority: customers are the priority until the day when customers can no longer be served or billed.

Security from the start of the Security by Design project

The implementation of a new tool requires project management, and it is at the time of project management that the security constraints (confidentiality, integrity, accessibility) of information must be taken into account, by defining the rules, organization, procedures and administration over time of these rules. This is called *Privacy by Design*. When these security constraints are taken into account from the beginning of the project, this avoids security breaches and compliance work once the project is completed or in use.

Moreover, at the time of design, options are also to be taken: for a given budget, what do we decide: to replace our door with an armored door, or with an unarmored door and an alarm system? Keep our identity and property documents and "family jewelry" in an easily accessible drawer, in an on-site safe or in an outdoor safe?

Each project, whether it is an email, a website, an application or software implementation, requires a prior analysis of the risks and solutions to be implemented. What data will be collected, exchanged, saved?

Is all this data useful? Which of these data are critical, sensitive, personal and confidential? Which ones should be protected? Who will have access to what? Are we in compliance with the law, the GDPR, in particular?

2.5.3. *The consequences of poor digital performance*

To ensure compliance with regulations, it is necessary to identify the data collected, verify that they are collected with the consent of users and that they are stored in secure conditions (in conjunction with the CISO). These new regulations, which focus on the end user, can be considered as opportunities for business.

Regardless of its size, the company is responsible: its managers and board of directors cannot rely on the CIO, the CISO or its IT service providers and must consider the organization, tools and processes to protect their strategic assets, their reputation and the (digital) trust that the company (the foundation or the association) enjoys from its customers and suppliers. Trust is slowly earned.

A computer attack, improper handling, poor data access management, lack of data classification, lack of training and awareness of the value of information can have serious consequences. The confidence of customers and suppliers will be permanently reduced.

It is recommended to use qualified service providers (especially for SMEs that do not have internal resources) to audit systems, organization and processes, raise awareness among internal and external stakeholders, recommend action plans and monitor their implementation.

The company can also use tools, which can be used to assess the level of compliance and cybersecurity of the company that the company is about to acquire, as well as to manage risk mitigation indicators and solutions in accordance with the company's operational and functional departments, all of which are data holders and therefore concerned by their protection.

2.5.4. *Cybersecurity*

Cyberspace is becoming a battleground: it is not science fiction, it is a reality. A factory can explode with a bomb and also with computer equipment, as industries are connected. A connection means the risk of a computer attack.

Cybersecurity involves many functions within organizations: general management, financial management, legal management, risk management, IT management, etc. Dialogue with project managers, sales or technical departments is essential: exchange on safety issues (what are the risks?) and solutions make it possible to become aware of potential safety problems and make informed decisions.

The CISO is a partner and guardian of the temple; he/she should not forget this function and ask for arbitration if he/she thinks that certain measures or systems do not comply with the company's rules. As with the security of property and people, IT security must be respected by all.

In terms of the future, do you see yourself being very confident, quite confident, quite worried or very worried? *Base: group (174 respondents)*

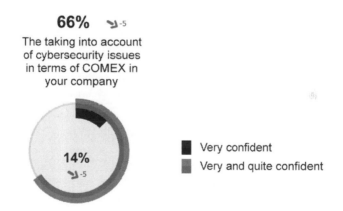

↗ ↘ Significant statistical change vs. 01/2018

Figure 2.3. *Background: CISOs are not very confident in the ability of their COMEX to take into account cybersecurity issues (source: according to CESIN). For a color version of this figure, see www.iste.co.uk/defreminville/cybersecurity.zip*

Internal governance is therefore essential: what are the roles and responsibilities of the various functions? Is the CISO dependent on the CIO? Who is the arbitrator in the event of a dispute? If the CISO is independent of the CIO, which is recommended, how does the CISO interact with the CIO, operations and functions, who does he/she report to and who arbitrates?

The intervention of the legal department, which ensures compliance with international regulations, laws and standards, is essential, as is that of the finance department, which will have to anticipate costs and productivity gains, finance investments and forecast additional security costs: the SOC (Security Operation Center), the CERT (Computer Emergency Response Team) or outsourced monitoring, depending on the size of the company and its activity, as well as training, intrusion tests and audits.

Internal governance requires clarifying roles and responsibilities, as well as setting up:

– security procedures and policies (an excellent CISO is not enough);

– a defense in depth: the door + alarm, rather than the armored door;

– Security by Design: security must be designed from the start of a project, it is much easier and less expensive than integrating it during the project, or once the project is completed;

– a continuity plan, to ensure that the company will be able to continue its sales, production and administration activities.

In this context, the CFO's concerns are very broad. The financial consequences of cybercrime for companies include financial assets, intellectual property, brand and Internet presence, reputation, business continuity, theft and illegal processing of personal data, disclosure of confidential information, fraud, ransom payments, data integrity, investigation costs in the event of an attack, the cost of litigation initiated by customers, employees, shareholders or partners.

The need for a real culture of cyber prevention concerns the entire economic fabric, particularly in the SMEs, which are less protected, are statistically the first targets and often the gateway to large companies.

For Swiss SMEs, for example, online security tests are provided by ICTswitzerland, as well as basic recommendations to protect companies.

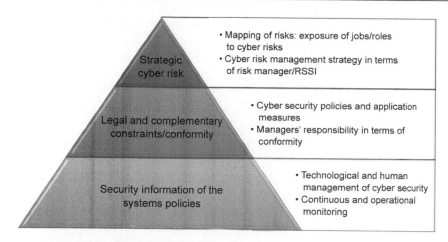

Figure 2.4.*Cyber-risk governance (source: Starboard Advisory)*

2.5.5. *Merger and acquisition transactions*

Finally, there is the particular case of mergers and acquisition transactions, which must be subject to cyber-specific due diligence.

Indeed, it is critical:

– to assess the quality of IT management, service providers, tools and processes, as well as the ability to detect and respond to incidents;

– to conduct an audit: cyber incidents, vulnerabilities, data recovery plans in the event of an attack, level of data protection, access management, at storage locations and during data transfers;

– to verify, in conjunction with the company's experts or external auditors, the cyber maturity of the "target", the nature of the data and their strategic value, compliance with IT regulations and standards, traces of IT incidents on the deep and darknet, cyber insurance policies;

– estimate the costs of securing systems, training technical teams and personnel (multifunctional and multi-site).

Once the acquisition is completed, it will be necessary to integrate, disseminate and enforce group procedures, map risks, implement the cybersecurity strategy to protect key assets, manage third parties and verify the existence of instructions to respond to incidents and ensure the company's resilience in the event of an attack.

2.5.6. *Governance and data protection, cybersecurity*

2.5.6.1. *Internal data*

To optimize data collection, updating and archiving efforts, as well as to ensure the quality of data essential for their analysis, it is necessary to define data governance: identify strategic and non-strategic data, collect the needs of businesses and functions, define the roles and responsibilities in the company for each data, as well as update rules (who, when, documentation) and access rules (writing, reading).

It is a real project, but if the company succeeds, it saves a lot of time and quality. This requires listening to the needs of all actors, understanding them and making compromises so that sharing is possible.

High discipline and the application of rigorous rules are essential if all actors are to have confidence in the quality of the data produced by others. This is a challenge for companies organized in silos, which do not share data with others, for fear of losing power, but it is a value-creating progress if data producers can act with a common objective.

If we add to this data governance, adequate governance of cybersecurity resources, involving IT functions, operational managers and finance, human resources and legal functions and a transformation of culture, the digital transformation will be successful.

2.5.6.2. *Customer data*

The collection of customer data can be done through several channels: relationships via sales teams, stores and websites. The pooling of all this data is a subject in its own right and requires the establishment of a sales organization that makes it possible to address the customer via different channels, without him/her feeling harassed, and, at the same time, it is necessary to ensure that all customers are in a common base.

The issue here is not to deal with this organization of commercial data, but rather to ensure the protection of such data, both for compliance and ethical reasons. This issue is discussed in the following chapters.

2.5.6.3. *Open data and personal data protection*

Administrations produce or collect data and must make them freely reusable. And, at the same time, they are subject to the GDPR. Even when anonymized, data can sometimes be attributed to a person, for example, by cross-referencing data.

This is an extremely sensitive subject, which, beyond the protection of information systems, requires specific data processing and precise controls to avoid processing that does not comply with the law.

2.5.6.4. *Public data – acute spying?*

Many cities and transport companies are setting up video surveillance systems. *Smart cities* collect data to improve car flows or energy consumption.

The objectives are often legitimate (security, cost reduction), sometimes only commercial (a Swiss start-up develops advertising panels that adapt to the profile of passersby). What is at stake is the consent of the data owner and the ability to protect the data: the providers are private companies. What do monitoring companies and IT service providers do with these data? Where do they store them? How long do they keep them? Who has access to it? How are they secured? Many questions arise. The responsibility for the confidentiality, integrity and security of these data is shared between the public and private spheres. The quality of the entire ecosystem is extremely important.

The City of Toronto has implemented many sensors and collected public and private data necessary for its operation, which could identify individuals and use the data for commercial purposes by the city's project company, a company in the Google galaxy, Sidewalk Labs.

What guarantees do Toronto residents have about the use of this data? How are they administered, by whom and for what purpose? What are the contractual and financial links between the city and the service provider? Are residents involved and do they have a voice? These are governance issues for cities.

– Cyber-risks are business risks: the company's reputation and the trust of customers/suppliers/partners are at stake.

– Present to the board of directors the figures and trends, the real cases in your sector of activity.

– Assess the financial risk of the cyber catastrophe scenario including the costs of restarting *business as usual.*

– Request a report from auditors or an independent, trusted expert.

– Draw attention to compliance, criminal liability and financial sanctions.

Box 2.1.*Cyber-risks are strategic risks: the five arguments
to convince the board of directors and management*

3

Risk Mapping

3.1. Cyber-risks

The rise of digital technology and digital transformation has brought new threats to the protection of data – strategic, personal or customer – as well as to the functioning of information, management or industrial systems and their protection.

The term "cyber-risk" is misleading. In reality, risks are business risks with an IT cause: the risk is not to sell, not to produce, not to be able to pay or be paid, because the training systems are blocked until a ransom is paid, or because the data is encrypted.

Reputation damage, whether as a result of data loss or online defamation, may also have an impact on the company's business. The landscape of cyber-risks is constantly changing, and they are difficult to quantify (lack of history).

There is no such thing as zero risk. The question is not "are we going to be victims of a cyber-attack?" but "when are we going to be victims of a cyber-attack?" Cyber-risk is a meta-risk, which affects all the company's functions.

Cyber-risks must be subject to specific due diligence: systems, skills, governance, budgets, quality of service providers, suppliers, subsidiaries, insurance and regular audits of cyber incidents, vulnerabilities and data recovery plans in the event of an attack.

The identification of strategic systems is not sufficient; the analysis of strategic data, the protection of this data, at storage locations and during data transfers, as well as access, are also essential parameters.

Assessing technical, human (internal and external: suppliers and service providers), financial and legal risks; assessing risks in cybersecurity governance and management involvement, the degree to which cybersecurity is taken into account in information systems and daily operations; setting up incident reporting; estimating the costs of securing systems and data, training technical teams and staff are part of the responsibilities of managers and boards.

The boards of directors have, among other things, a legal obligation to monitor the effectiveness of the company's risk management system and will in particular ensure the implementation of an action plan to remedy these risks (by setting priorities).

Operations managers must therefore be aware of the risks, provide the company with a global risk management system (ERM, Enterprise Risk Management), entrust its coordination to the risk manager (for large companies), whose mission is to implement remediation and prevention policies, as well as the transfer to insurance, which contribute to the company's resilience.

The control of cyber-risks is complex; cybersecurity is a transversal subject that requires a risk governance approach, assumed responsibilities and the involvement of all stakeholders. The coherence of managerial and technological approaches is a key factor for success.

Some sectors of activity (BtoC or health, for example) are more exposed than others. Each company must implement an information system security policy (ISSP): guarantee the accessibility of the system, its proper functioning, the confidentiality of information and its integrity.

Far from being reserved only for critical environments, the challenge will ultimately be to certify trusted systems and products.

Cyber-risk is no longer a technical risk but a business risk, and it is therefore necessary to define a governance and organization of the company's cybersecurity resources, involving IT functions, operations managers and support functions. This is a prerequisite for the company's resilience.

The company, whatever its activity, must put in place processes that guarantee confidentiality, integrity, data security, appropriate governance (roles and responsibilities: who has access, who gives access to which data, who can transfer it and to whom, who keeps it, etc.), the classification of these data (degree of confidentiality, sensitivity, interest for the business) and therefore the right level of protection, to be decided with the CISO.

The main mission of cybersecurity teams is to protect digital information in all its dimensions – personal and strategic – and to advise operational departments in the development of new products or services based on the data owned by the company, while ensuring their protection. Maximizing the potential of the data used can also result in financial gains, productivity gains and improved employee efficiency.

3.2. The context

More than one organization in two does not regularly perform cyber resilience testing, according to a Ponemon Institute survey. Seventy-seven percent (82% in France) of IT professionals surveyed stated that they do not consistently apply a Computer Security Incident Response Plan (CSIRP) throughout the company. However, the irregular frequency of IT security tests – cyber resilience – can be costly for companies.

Digital technology, the speed of exchanges, the size of companies and the internationalization of operations have led to the loss of sovereignty of states, a loss of control over information flows in large companies, the disappearance of national rules concerning many previously classified information and a transformation of uses; it is now the reign of all-round exchange sharing, including on social networks, and transparency: native digital people see transparency as a solution to the world's dysfunction.

The speed of operations, the reduction in staff, the separation of tasks, the complexity of organizations and the lack of proximity often make employee engagement less important and the understanding of the issues less important. Criminals enjoy themselves. The consequences are first and foremost economic.

3.3. Vulnerabilities

A vulnerability is a security breach that can be exploited by a criminal. Some vulnerabilities are zero-day, i.e. known, but for which there is no patch. Some vulnerabilities are known, and there are patches to be applied.

Automated analysis software, based on databases of known vulnerabilities, can be used to identify potential vulnerabilities in networks, applications, servers, systems or equipment. Once the analyses have been conducted, the tool reports on all the problems detected and suggests actions to close the gaps. The most advanced tools will help to decide whether to correct or accept risk based on the impact on business operations and security. The analysis can be integrated with a SIEM (Security Information and Event Management) solution to provide a more complete analysis.

Penetration tests are also a complement to vulnerability analysis and allow us to know whether the vulnerability can be exploited and with what impacts. They also make it possible to identify software, application or other vulnerabilities and to complete the list of zero-day vulnerabilities and known vulnerabilities.

The main objective is to assess the risks and establish the corrective action plan. As IT security teams' resources are generally limited, they will have to plan their actions according to the priorities defined in conjunction with the company's (or public organization's) operational and functional managers:

– regarding a zero-day vulnerability, it may be decided to isolate applications or parts of the system, and perform additional checks, pending a patch. The impacts will thus be limited, in the event of an attack;

– concerning known vulnerabilities, a corrective action program can be established based on priorities defined with the company's businesses and functions, and regulatory requirements (priorities are defined according to the probability of the occurrence of the attack on the identified vulnerabilities and the estimated impact).

It is very important to prioritize actions with operations managers, who must be aware of the risks, understand them and be active in implementing solutions or taking risks, in coordination with safety managers.

3.3.1. *Fraud against the president*

Fraud against the president represents 480 million euros per year in France. It consists of cybercriminals posing as managers of a company, usually by asking an accountant or treasurer to make a transfer abroad for a substantial amount (from 1 to 20 million depending on the size of the target company) for a very confidential and very urgent operation (acquisition of a company). Thanks to good information about the company, its organization, its processes and projects, by "playing" on the fear or ego of employees, during holiday periods, or during changes of managers, scammers manage to get operations done, which should normally not be authorized if the processes were followed.

Pathé was the victim of a fraud of more than 19 million euros committed in March 2018, intended for an alleged acquisition in Dubai. Thousands of companies were victims: KPMG in 2012 for €7.2 million, Airbus in Germany for €3 million, Michelin, Intermarché, Coca-Cola also, while a record €42 million was diverted at the beginning of the year to an Austrian aerospace equipment manufacturer called FACC.

Insurance companies do not consider these frauds as cyber frauds, although there is often identity theft "false emails"; however, they are facilitated by digital means: an order transmitted by email, a telephone call reproducing the manager's voice using a "vocoder", and reduced controls by banks.

3.3.2. *Supplier fraud*

Supplier fraud is quite simple: the fraudster contacts a company's supplier, posing as the company's accountant or auditor and asking him/her for information on invoices awaiting payment. The fraudster then contacts the company, posing as its supplier, and asks to change the bank account. He/she then notifies you of a change of bank account and sends the supplier's letterhead invoices with the new account number and telephone details.

Like fraud against the president, supplier fraud is facilitated by a dispersed organization, accounting that is remote from operations (outsourced shared services, sometimes in distant countries), the ability to mislead accounting teams with emails (identity theft), fake documents sent by email (they are no longer paper originals), a lack of training on procedures, traps to avoid and checks to perform.

Accounting departments are often the last wheel of the carriage; the company tries to save, restructure, digitalize, but pay attention to the quality of the teams, their knowledge of the company's partners and their understanding of the activities.

Digitization must be accompanied by clear training and processes: counter-call to the supplier, identity verification (by telephone and email), verification with the bank, signature of a manager for validation of the new bank account, limitation of communication of information on the Internet and by email.

Fraudsters are very imaginative and persistent and almost always exploit the human fault line.

3.3.3. *Other economic impacts*

What was the impact of cyberattacks on your business?
Basis: group (174 respondents)/several results possible

Significant statistical development vs 01/2018

Figure 3.1. *History: the greater impact of cyber-attacks on the business of targeted companies (source: CESIN). For a color version of this figure, see www.iste.co.uk/defreminville/cybersecurity.zip*

Apart from fraud, companies also experience (source Accenture):

– disclosures of confidential information (63%): loss of intellectual property, competitive advantage, customer data;

– a negative impact on reputation (38%);

– operating losses (30%);

– direct financial losses (28%);

– financial extortion with ransom (17%).

In 2015, half a billion pieces of personal information were lost or stolen worldwide.

The points of attack are multiplying: not only the networks of small and large companies but also our telephones, tablets, connected objects, fitness bracelets and refrigerators to automated metro trains are all targets.

Cybercrime costs $445 million a year, while natural disasters have represented "only" $160 million in damage on average over the past 10 years worldwide.

The financial and reputational consequences for companies therefore concern:

– financial assets – through fraud, theft and extortion: "president's fraud", which evolves through artificial intelligence (recent example of identity theft through voice reproduction), fraudulent change of supplier account;

– intellectual property and trade secrets – through spying;

– the brand and its presence on the Internet – through boycott, defamation and damage to the image (modification of the website);

– business continuity – through sabotage or disruption of operations (website and customer services, production);

– theft and illegal processing of personal data;

– the disclosure of confidential information (internal instructions, strategic data, mergers and acquisitions, etc.);

– the ransoms;

– data integrity;

– the costs of investigation in the event of an attack and disputes initiated by customers, employees, shareholders or partners and defense costs;

– reputation: more than three-quarters of customers have little or no confidence in the companies and suppliers that process and manage their personal data. Ethics, in its legal and societal components, must therefore be considered as a strategic asset for companies.

3.4. Legal risks

3.4.1. *Class actions*

In June 2017, Anthem, Inc. one of the largest US healthcare companies, agreed to pay a record $115 million to settle class actions following a data breach involving the personal information of nearly 80 million customers in 2015.

There have been a number of other important data breach regulations in recent years. In 2016 and 2017, Home Depot settled the class actions based on the violation for $19.5 million. Similarly, in 2015 and 2016, Target paid $105 million to settle data breach class actions.

In 2014, a Morrisons senior internal auditor downloaded a file containing nearly 100,000 personal data of Morrisons employees, including names, addresses, dates of birth, telephone numbers, bank account numbers and salaries. The court found the company liable, even though it had cybersecurity controls, and the offense was caused by an employee acting on his/her own initiative. In British labor law, vicarious liability refers to the liability of the employer for the actions of its employee.

On October 8, 2018, a shareholder filed a security class action against the Chinese group Huazhu. This legal action, linked to a data breach, has a number of interesting features. Huazhu operates hotels in China. Its shares are listed on the Nasdaq. On August 28, 2018, Shanghai police issued a statement on social media stating that they had been alerted to a possible data breach in the company. According to media reports, "nearly 500 million pieces of information from the group had been published in an online message": 123 million pieces of registration data on the official Huazhu website, such as name, mobile number, identity number and connection ID code; 240 million pieces of hotel stay data, such as name, credit card number, mobile phone number, arrival and departure times, consumption amount and room number. In its statement of September 17, the company added that "the police arrested the suspects who posted the reported message on a dark web forum in order to sell certain data". The attempted sale was unsuccessful.

On October 8, 2018, a shareholder of Huazhu filed a class action in the Central District of California against Huazhu and the company's chief executive officer. The complaint alleges that the company's share price decreased by more than 12% during the five trading days following the announcement of the customer data leak.

The complaint alleged a lack of transparency of the company toward investors, that the company did not have adequate security measures to protect customer information, that it would be exposed to an increased risk of litigation and higher costs. The information provided by the company to shareholders about the company's activities, operations and prospects was substantially false or even misleading. The number of class actions is certainly likely to increase in the future.

3.4.2. Sanctions by the CNIL and the ICO

With the introduction of the GDPR in May 2018, 2018 was a record year, particularly in terms of the number of complaints (+32%). The CNIL (*Commission nationale de l'informatique et des libertés*) is "clearly identified as a source of reference information for professionals and the general public".

A third of the 11,077 complaints lodged concerned data published on the Internet, 21% concerned prospecting, followed by human resources and banks. We can also mention the remote viewing of images from video devices, in particular by the employer, pointing to a risk of excessive surveillance of employees, the installation of cameras in care units, thus filming people vulnerable for their "security", the desire of customers of banks or online content services to use their right to the portability of their data, the security of their personal data, and not only on the Internet, fears about the data to which mobile applications can have access in a smartphone. Approximately 20% of complaints are now the subject of European cooperation.

The CNIL carried out 310 inspections in 2018. In the majority of cases, its intervention resulted in compliance by the organization: 10 financial penalties (nine public and seven concerning breaches of personal data security) and one non-public warning were issued in 2018.

British Airways announced on July 8, 2019, that it was expected to pay a fine of £183 million (€204 million) to the UK's Information Commissioner's Office (ICO) following the theft in 2018 of hundreds of thousands of customers' data, including their name, address and credit card data, including number, expiry date and three-digit security code.

The ICO estimated that about 500,000 customers had seen their data "computed" and attributed it to "poor security systems in the company". "People's personal data must remain so", said ICO Commissioner Elizabeth Denham.

"When you are given personal data, you must protect it. Those who do not will be prosecuted by the ICO to verify that they have taken the appropriate measures", she said.

The amount of the fine imposed by the ICO represents 1.5% of British Airways' annual turnover in 2017.

The method used by the attackers allows the data to be sucked up by injecting computer code into the site's reservation pages. This code records mouse movements and clicks on payment pages, allowing hackers to reconstruct the information entered by users.

3.5. The objectives of risk mapping

The main objective is to take appropriate measures to ensure the company's sustainability and therefore its performance.

Risk mapping must be based on the company's strategic objectives. It must primarily focus on critical systems, information and processes.

As we have already seen, the company is vulnerable, because connected to its environment, there is no such thing as zero risk, and the aim is not to transform the company into a fortified castle with several levels of ramparts.

The security system has three objectives:

– data security: data protection, data archiving (digital and paper), individual and/or shared archiving, file (in emails or folders) and email classification, backups (frequency, quality, integrity), retention period and company rules to be respected;

– confidentiality: the identification of confidential data, the choice of appropriate communication or sharing methods (email, meeting, paper, SMS, social networks) according to the subjects and the level of confidentiality or legal risk (in the event of a procedure, emails leave traces [too much writing]);

– integrity: the management of access rights (reading, input, administration) and the documentation that justifies the quality of the data.

3.6. The different methods of risk analysis

Different methods of risk analysis on the information system exist: the important thing is to appropriate a method, adapt it to the company, involve the different functions and/or operations of the company and ensure that it does not become a routine. The aim is not to follow the method, the aim is to make it a tool for exchanging information, identifying major risks and making decisions to remedy these risks, clarify responsibilities (who is in charge of what and when) and transfer certain risks to insurance, according to the conditions proposed by insurance companies.

In England, CRAMM is a risk analysis method developed by the British government organization CCTA (Central Communication and Telecommunication Agency). This is the risk analysis method preferred by the British government, but it is also used by many other countries.

In its document "*Norme minimale pour améliorer sa résilience informatique*" ("Minimum Standard to Improve IT Resilience"), the DEFR (*Département fédéral de l'économie, de la formation et de la recherche de la confédération suisse*) distinguishes between industrial control systems (ICSs) and information and communication technologies (ICTs) and recommends the application of international standards (ISO, COBIT), as well as the NIST (National Institute of Standards and Technology) framework, consisting of:

– identify;

– protect;

– detect;

– react;

– recover.

The United States uses OCTAVE (Operationally Critical Threat, Asset, and Vulnerability Evaluation), developed by Carnegie Mellon University.

Internationally, ISO/IEC 27005 is used, which is an international standard that meets the requirements of the ISO/IEC 27001 certification step by step. It is the most recent standard and is easily applicable because it is pragmatic.

In France, the EBIOS method (expression of needs and identification of security objectives) developed by the *Agence nationale de la sécurité des systèmes d'information* (ANSSI) is most often used. This method can be used to map the risks of the company and its ecosystem, as well as to manage the risks of an IT project, or of a product or service developed by the company.

This method has several advantages: it is pragmatic and operational, it involves the business lines, it gives working groups the opportunity to inventory the IT systems used, to imagine where threats can come from, to describe the feared events, to define a plan of measures for the risks identified by the business lines, the IT department and the IT security department, starting with the most likely (inaccessible data, websites, courier services, production stoppages, fraud). The synthesis will be presented to the executive management so that it can understand, arbitrate, prioritize and possibly release resources (human and financial) for the implementation of the proposed strategy.

All these methods must be adapted to the sector and size of the company. It is important, whatever the company, public organization, association or foundation, to adopt this method and to have the various actors in the company regularly assess the IT risks that could hinder the availability, integrity or confidentiality of the systems.

It is also essential that this risk management work does not become routine, updating what was done six months or a year ago, without challenging the risk hierarchy, threats and scenarios. It is therefore necessary to modify the composition of the teams, by keeping a few people who will be able to recall the reasoning made during previous analyses, and by including internal or external people, who will have a new eye, a critical look and a new vision of the issues.

3.7. Risk assessment (identify)

Impact of cyber incidents		Probability of cyber incidents	
Assets at risk	Loss of	Vulnerabilities	Threats
Intangible assets: intellectual property; reputation; conformity	Confidentiality	Culture and staff	Dissatisfied employees
			Human error
			Insider trading
			Activism
Material assets: financial; stocks; systems of production; infrastructure facility	Integrity	Organization and processes	Criminality
			Action of suppliers or partners
			Sabotage
Common good: personal safety; privacy; personal freedoms	Availability	Technology and infrastructure	Spying
			Terrorism
			Cyberwarfare

Table 3.1. *2017 World Economic Forum Risk Framework*

3.7.1. *The main actors*

It is essential that the business lines and main users of a system, software, application or process understand where the IT risks are located, which can affect the functioning of their operational activities. The first step is to imagine what the impacts would be on the company in terms of operations (sales, production, logistics), finance (loss of turnover, fraud), law (disputes) and reputation (quality problem, inability to deliver, health problem) if an information system were corrupt, or the quality of data deteriorated as a result of an attack, or data was not available due to the activation of a ransom.

Operations managers also have a vision of potential threats, internal or external, that could act in a malicious manner.

In other words, what are the consequences of a three-day blockade of the website and the inability to sell its products for a consumer goods distribution company? What would be the impacts of a quality control problem (of malicious or non-malicious origin) on a dairy production industry that could lead to consumer food poisoning? What would be the consequences for a law firm or a tax firm of no longer being able to access files, which have been completely dematerialized, for several weeks?

Risk managers, IT managers and IT security managers cannot be the only people in charge of risk assessment. These assessments should be systematically co-signed by operations managers and IT security managers, and then consolidated or even prioritized by risk managers for large companies or by senior management.

3.7.2. *The steps*

The first action consists of an inventory of equipment and resources, which will also provide an understanding of the system architecture, including connections between industrial systems and the company network (which must be limited and protected), an inventory of workstations (which must be configured in a consistent manner and comply with common rules) and a complete overview of internal and external information flows.

The ISO2700x family of standards defines "assets" as any element having a value for the organization: primary or production assets (upstream logistics, manufacturing, downstream logistics, marketing and sales, services, processes, information) and secondary assets (servers, software, networks, purchasing, research and development, skills, IT). Prioritizing the assets to be protected is the first step.

The physical security of this equipment is intended to prevent malicious intrusions to access, steal, modify, destroy or damage information, whether the equipment is fixed (servers, for example) or mobile (computers, telephones, etc.).

It also aims to protect them from accidents such as fires, floods or acts of terrorism. The system may not always be protected, but the information can be duplicated and backed up on different sites and systems.

This first step is essential: without a clear understanding of strategic assets (tangible and intangible), strategic processes, security policies, governance (who is responsible for what), company IT equipment (hardware, network, software) and security equipment and/or solutions, as well as internal and external skills, solutions to prioritize risks and provide solutions are unlikely to be appropriate.

3.8. Protecting

The protection of systems and data requires the implementation of:

– security tools related to the network (firewall, anti-spam), detection (monitoring and log logs), access (authentication) and access management (who has access to what);

– security rules: passwords, access to websites, USB key, Wi-Fi;

– control (regular audits, intrusion tests, application of rules);

– training throughout the chain, from top to bottom and bottom to top, not to mention the many temporary or permanent external staff. Indeed, the major risk is between the chair and the table: credulity, lack of vigilance, incompetence, negligence, etc. Training from the moment of recruitment is a good practice.

3.9. Detecting

It is rare that a burglary or bank robbery takes place without prior identification of the premises, habits, schedules, access possibilities and conditions, holiday dates, change of managers.

Surveillance therefore makes it possible to act before pirates attack. It is necessary to identify connection attempts, abnormal data leaks (harmless at first, they will increase if no one notices anything, as in the case of financial fraud). When external service providers are authorized to connect to the network, to information systems, it is important to set up special procedures and to be able to detect unauthorized connections. As companies are better protected, attackers go through connected suppliers or subcontractors.

Incidents can come from different sources, tools or people. It is therefore necessary to analyze the data (including access) and organize these alerts.

Care must be taken not to neglect the sharing of information with other companies, circles of safety managers and service providers, which makes it possible to improve the alert system.

Beware of holiday and festive periods, as these are the preferred times for attackers.

3.10. Reacting

Do you have an intervention plan in case of an attack?

Is this intervention plan known to the company's teams? Do they know who to notify in case of an anomaly? Do they know how to react? Who to call? On which number? Unplug, deactivate the connection?

For obscure reasons, security is too often in the hands of a few people, instead of being everyone's business. How many companies have issued IT security instructions to all staff in the event of receiving a fraudulent email (destroy it? forward it to security?), in the event of opening a fraudulent attachment (notify who? Unplug your computer? Disconnect your mobile?) or in the event of ransom messages or suspicious phone calls?

An IT service provider calls you and "on instructions from the IT department" comes to perform maintenance operations, or take control of your computer remotely.

A president receives an email about updating his Wikipedia; he rushes to look at what Wikipedia will publish about him, proud to be part of this prestigious club. He clicks and the attacker has managed to break through; he will read his emails for weeks, months or even years.

Avoiding attacks is not possible; avoiding bad reactions is possible. Vigilance is based on the awareness of these different scenarios, the implementation of procedures and the application of these procedures by all. Some managers, particularly in France, consider that the procedures are applicable for all except them.

Mistakes are human; no one is safe. The question is: how can we prevent the error from having no impact? And what to do immediately?

The incident must be understood: where did the attack come from? What are the consequences? What was the objective? What lessons can be learned from this? What are the vulnerabilities and how can they be fixed? Was the response plan effective and how could it be improved?

3.11. Restoring

Restoration is a major step; it consists of restarting systems, services and making data accessible again, with the initial level of confidentiality and integrity.

3.12. Decentralized mapping

3.12.1. *The internal threat*

As already mentioned several times, the threat is very often internal, sometimes malicious, often negligent or misinformed. Seventy-five percent of internal incidents are reported to be accidental and unintentional.

Former employees (or those in the departure phase) are a point of vigilance: one out of four internal incidents comes from a (former) malicious employee. How to identify them and prevent them from committing malicious acts?

Do the functions (IT, human resources, legal and compliance) work together and with the business lines to establish a culture of cybersecurity and accountability? Has regular training been implemented to know the instructions and recognize threats?

What are the most effective methods of awareness and training? Games? E-learning with augmented reality and adapted to the company's environment? Fraudulent fake email campaigns sent to all staff?

Written procedures distributed to all staff on data, systems, and mobile equipment?

Are cyber incidents reported spontaneously (safe environment)?

What human resources policies in terms of recruitment, training, mobility and understanding of cyber issues transfer from one function to another? When a person leaves the company voluntarily or not, what precautions are taken on the data they hold and process?

Are access controls, encryption, backups or traffic monitoring in place and effective?

What is the legal environment regarding the confidentiality of company information? The employment contract? The internal regulations? Is the legal department involved in the cyber plan for internal threats?

Hackers know how to identify the employees to target: system administrators, with important privileges, IT helpdesk staff, management committee members. Trapped by highly targeted phishing attacks, they are an effective way to access the company's infrastructure.

Proper administration of access rights and the application of the principle of least privilege (rights of a user strictly limited to the needs of his/her work) remain essential to minimize the risks following the compromise of a user account: the fewer rights he/she has, the less effective the attack will be.

Third parties, service providers, suppliers and subcontractors are more difficult to manage than employees, and must be subject to special treatment.

3.12.2. *Industrial risks*

Industrial systems are much less secure than IT installations. Technologies are very heterogeneous in industrial environments. Network access is not always listed, data is not encrypted, systems are still configured with default passwords, while the lack of a security culture in industry makes it easier for attackers.

The life cycles of industrial installations are long; so, they are more vulnerable to new risks, and the business links/security managers are sometimes (often?) too weak.

Hervé Guillou stated this in 2016:

> The cyber-risk for the company is of a transversal nature. But what we see is that it is unfortunately all too often associated with the company's general IT and much less so with its industrial production environment, and almost never (except in banks) with the company's products and services (operational IT). All too often, the cybersecurity manager of a company, when there is one, is the CIO/Chief Information Officer himself or, even worse, someone attached to him. It doesn't work![1]

Multidisciplinary problems

Figure 3.2. *Cyber-risk: a business risk (source: Naval Group)*

---

1 HEC Gouvernance round table on October 13, 2016.

Targets

Three target IT
domains are more
and more vulnerable
and interconnectivity
is increasing

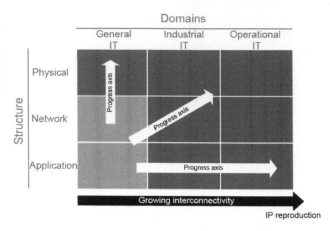

Figure 3.3. *The interconnectivity of IT domains (source: Naval Group). For a color version of this figure, see www.iste.co.uk/defreminville/cybersecurity.zip*

The CIO is in charge of general IT most often, and much more rarely industrial IT and never operational IT, which have very different technological bases. Moreover, it is often "schizophrenic" insofar as the CIO is under constant budgetary pressure and therefore tends to focus on what is immediately visible to its users to the detriment of what is not visible, cybersecurity.

In addition, the "all is well, Mr. President" syndrome is quite widespread in this area.

3.12.3. *Suppliers, subcontractors and service providers*

Many questions arise and deserve to be addressed to limit the risks.

What visibility do we have on the cyber exposure of the supply chain and all third parties with whom the company works and exchanges data? Who is involved in the decisions? How can we integrate the supply chain dimension into cyber-risk management? How can we integrate cyber requirements into subcontracting and service contracts? Is it possible and/or expensive to set up cyber vulnerability tests and intrusion tests at our suppliers? How to strengthen access points in our suppliers' networks?

What clauses have we included in contracts with suppliers? What about the requirements for compliance with ISO standards and industry regulations? Are their digital risks covered by insurance? In the event of cyber incidents, what compensation will be paid by the supplier, if the latter is found liable? Do we have the right to audit its systems, processes and organization? What is its ability to keep information confidential?

The supply chain of companies is increasingly digitalized and therefore vulnerable due to its multiple interconnections and the growing number of actors that can generate cascading reactions.

Industrial environments operated independently of traditional office IT including email and web browsing. The new generations of robots now use the same networks and are therefore exposed to cybercrime. Saint-Gobain and Renault were attacked via office automation, which then infected the assembly and distribution lines.

It is therefore essential to measure the "pros" (performance, speed, etc.) and the "cons" (impacts of cyber threats) when digitizing industrial sites.

The objectives of the IT Department (IT performance, facilitation of information exchanges) and the CISO (securing systems and data) are in constant conflict and must be decided by the business lines and therefore by the industrial management as far as the supply chain is concerned. Businesses are responsible: they must therefore understand and decide according to the advantages and disadvantages of the proposed IT solutions.

This is one of the reasons why cybersecurity is a topic for decision makers.

3.12.4. *Connected objects*

A connected object has a digital identity, is equipped with sensors, which can transmit a signal, and is connected to the Internet. Security breaches can come from the object itself, the Wi-Fi network, as well as from the user, who does not change the password and does not update it.

Connected objects are the new gateway for attackers: computers were previously the only targets. For example, a security breach was recently discovered in the Bluetooth protocol that would allow you to take control of a device such as a wireless speaker or even a smartphone to extract data from it.

The consequences range from invasion of privacy, device takeover (e.g. camera), theft of personal data, identity theft and breakdowns, which can have serious consequences.

There are many examples of vulnerabilities related to connected objects:

– the new unsecured electricity meters installed in Spain allowed power cuts at the owners' premises to be traced back to the power plants through a cascade infection system;

– video surveillance cameras can be transformed into botnets, a network of machines used without the owner's knowledge to carry out denial of service attacks against companies (simultaneous sending thousands of requests in order to saturate servers within companies).

The development of connected objects is a growing opportunity for cybercriminals, as security is not the priority in the design of connected objects for the general public: it represents a cost, and users are not willing to pay more for a more secure object.

Industrially connected objects constitute a new attack surface and therefore new security risks, which must be taken into account in companies.

Mirai malware is known in this field: devices infected by Mirai search the Internet for IP addresses corresponding to connected objects. Once spotted, they are used to attack a target and are difficult for the target to spot.

The democratization of connected objects should give rise to new scams or new possibilities to undermine cryptocurrency. It will also give rise to new regulations: Margot James, the British Digital Secretary, introduced a bill in May 2019 to counter cyber-attacks. This new law will require all devices connected to the Internet, such as household appliances, webcams or smart thermostats, to be sold with a unique password, whereas they are currently sold with hard-coded default passwords. The law will also require manufacturers to provide a public contact point so that researchers and hackers can submit vulnerabilities of the connected devices. They will also have to inform consumers of the safety update times for each device. Finally, this law will lead to the creation of a new labeling system in the form of security by design, to ensure that products have integrated safety features from the design stage.

In your opinion, what is the main challenge for the RSSI concerning IoT (Internet of Things) in business?
Basis: group (174)

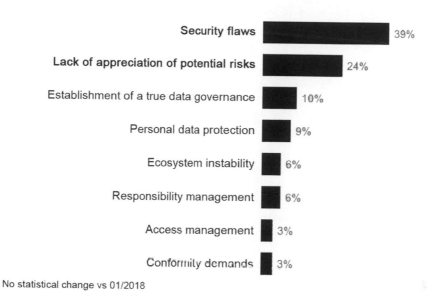

No statistical change vs 01/2018

Figure 3.4. *Security breaches, the most striking*
feature of IoTs (source: according to CESIN)

Connected toys

"There are a whole series of serious problems concerning children's toys, connected watches and intelligent robots, with the possibility of recording and transferring data", explains Ursula Pachl, Deputy Director General of the European Consumer Organization (BEUC).

Anyone within a 15 meter radius can connect to the "my friend Cayla" doll, the report explains. "Simply turn on the Bluetooth on your phone and press the doll's name to be able to play any audio file via the doll, which then turns into a remotely connected speaker".

This means that a stranger outside the doll's home would have the ability to connect, extract the data contained in the toy's memory and inject their own messages into it. "So a stranger can take control of the toy to communicate with your child", concludes Ursula Pachl.

Voice assistants

Tens of millions of people use voice assistants to find and play music, turn on the light or ask for directions.

According to a Bloomberg report dated April 11, 2019, Amazon.com employs hundreds of people worldwide to improve the Alexa voice assistant. These people listen to the recordings from the users' homes or offices, and are then integrated into the software, in order to improve the understanding of the human voice in different languages and thus provide a better response to the request.

Employees sign confidentiality agreements, and Amazon has procedures in place to ensure that the system is not diverted from its purpose and that employees can either cut passages from the recording or share information when they witness particular situations (people at risk, abuse, crime, etc.) or have access to confidential information (credit card number, health, political or religious opinions, etc.).

According to Amazon, employees cannot identify the people they are listening to. But why has this voice assistant been commercialized when it is not yet working well?

The reputation of the company that integrates these voice assistants could be impacted: Orange for its connected speakers, Qualcomm and its headsets, US Bank and its banking services, Legrand and its switches. Are end-users informed? Did Amazon's listening take place, in agreement with the company selling the product? Has the final customer given his or her consent and is he or she alerted each time he or she is registered?

What are the rules of confidentiality (link between the user and the registration)?

Is the customer well informed of the ability to say no to listening and does the company that integrates the voice assistant into its products have the ability to audit, to ensure that Amazon does not listen to those who have said no?

What are the current rules regarding data? Are the recordings transmitted to Amazon studios securely, and are they stored (and for how long) or destroyed?

Beyond compliance issues, these are questions that arise for users. Amazon, in its marketing presentations and privacy policies, does not clearly explain that the recordings will be listened to by its teams.

Users have the ability to disable the ability to record their voices, but Amazon indicates that the recordings can still be analyzed "manually". These are transmitted with the owner's first name and the serial number of the device.

Amazon is not the only company to market this type of device: Google Home and HomePod appeared before Alexa. A total of 78 million voice assistants were sold in 2018.

Security measures for connected objects

A minimum of security can be provided by the user, individual or professional: close unnecessary ports and avoid default passwords at all costs, accept automatic updates as soon as their device is switched on, avoid unencrypted communications, a technical capacity available today on very inexpensive systems. Sellers of connected objects should draw users' attention to these issues. California is the first state in the United States to adopt a law on connected objects.

This law will come into force in 2020, will require any manufacturer of connected objects to provide it with functions to "protect the device and the information it contains against unauthorized access, destruction, use, modification or disclosure", and will apply to all objects sold in California.

The device must have a unique password, and the user must define a password when logging in for the first time. There are no longer generic default identifiers that are too easy for cyber pirates to guess.

3.13. Insurance

Insurance is beginning to offer a response to the many potential harms of cyber-risk: data recovery costs, crisis management assistance, image recovery assistance, cost of corporate liability claims by those who have had their personal data hacked.

In addition, has your company subscribed to cyber insurance?
Basis: group (174 respondents)

50% ⬈+10   **10%**   **18%**

have subscribed to
a cyber insurance

are going
to subscribe

envisage subscribing
long-term

⬈ ⬊ Significant statistical change vs 01/2018

Figure 3.5. *Companies are increasingly subscribing to cyber insurance (source: according to CESIN). For a color version of this figure, see www.iste.co.uk/defreminville/cybersecurity.zip*

The insurance of these risks is not always implemented. The value of stolen data is complicated to assess, and the insurance policy will not prevent attacks but will intervene to deal with the financial and other consequences of cyber-attacks.

It is therefore recommended to check whether the contract covers cyber events, the information system and the cost of business interruption, the audit to understand the facts, the reconstruction of what has been destroyed, damage to third parties, and image risk.

In 2018, only 24% of companies had taken out insurance related to cybersecurity risks. Updating the insurance contract will verify the quality of the protection system, security policies and potential vulnerabilities.

The cyber-risk landscape is constantly changing. Cyber-risks are complex and difficult to quantify, particularly because of the rapidly changing technological environment and the lack of historical data on cyber-claims.

As Denis Kessler, CEO of Scor Insurance and Reinsurance Company, states in a document published in April 2017:

> In view of the risk universe, there are three type of risks: 'Acts of God', which relate to natural events, 'Acts of men', which are the result of technological progress, and 'Acts of the devil', which include crimes, acts of war and terrorist attacks. Cyber-risk is a perfect example of how complex risks can be today, as cyber is recent, intangible, invisible, cross-border, and rapidly developing, at a pace with technology. In a cyber context, 'Acts of men' include accidental events with unintended damages or consequences, while 'Acts of the devil' refer to cybercrime.[2]

It is therefore recommended to check that we can answer these questions: does my contract cover cyber events and is the information system covered by my contract? Does the insurance cover all the consequences just mentioned?

The outcome of the dispute between Mondelez and Zurich Re is interesting to follow. This case may indeed set a precedent:

– Mondelez lost 1,700 servers and 24,000 computers infected with NotPetya malware in 2017. The insurance contract subscribed by Mondelez stipulates that it is covered for "all risks of physical loss or material damage", as well as for "physical loss or damage caused to electronic data, programs, or software, including loss or damage caused by the malicious introduction of an instruction or code generated by a machine";

– Mondelez, which owns the Toblerone, Oreo and Cadbury brands, claims $100 million from Zurich American Insurance Company, Zurich Re's American subsidiary;

– Zurich Re first offered Mondelez compensation of USD 10 million and finally rejected any compensation, invoking an exclusion clause in its

---

2 According to the Scor Conference 2017: "Cyber risk on the rise: from intangible threat to tangible (re)insurance solutions".

property damage insurance policy for damage caused by "a hostile act or act of war" by "a sovereign government or power";

– this massive cyber-attack – of the ransomware type – had indeed been attributed to an action by Russian hackers aimed at destabilizing the Ukrainian government, although the Russian government has always denied being at the origin. An argument adopted by Zurich American Insurance Company, which considers NotPetya as "an act of war";

– the Mondelez Group is suing Zurich American Insurance Company.

If Zurich Re is not convicted, this will have an immediate impact on all companies, which will not seek to transfer cyber-risks to insurance or will seek to obtain from their insurance company that the consequences of acts of war are covered.

3.14. Non-compliance risks and ethics

The risks of non-compliance are quite recent: they mainly date back to the entry into force of the GDPR in May 2018, even if other laws such as the Data Protection Act in France or the LPD in Switzerland already regulated the processing, automatic or not, of personal data.

The GDPR takes into account the considerable digital developments since the emergence of the Internet in 1989, the collection of data by digital societies and the exponential growth in the use of such data for economic, political or criminal purposes.

The risks of non-compliance are therefore significant for companies, and sanctions can be significant.

In addition, consumers will be increasingly sensitive to the use made of their data, and the trust they place in their supplier will depend on both respect for their consent (or non-consent), transparency on the collection and processing of this data, and finally on the protection measures put in place by these companies.

– What are our five greatest vulnerabilities? Share with your CISO the five greatest risks that your IS (information system) poses to your activity, the vulnerabilities that you are concerned about and that you would like to cover (cloud, Shadow IT, etc.).

– Was the last cyber-attack in our risk mapping? Have you validated the mapping and do you know the risks your company is taking? How resilient would your company be to the latest published attack? Are you ready?

– When was the last time we had a security audit? What are the auditors' opinions on cloud solutions, compliance with our company's risk matrix, Shadow IT and unclassified team uses?

– Are we prepared for a cyber crisis? Fire drills arc often organized. Why not do the same with the IS? Have you ever done it before? Do you have a plan in case of a major attack?

– How arc we legally protected? In the event of poor IS protection, your civil and criminal liability as a manager may be engaged – especially in the event of disclosure of personal data. Do you know your risk exposure? Have you discussed this with your CISO, your legal representative or your external counsel?

Box 3.1. *The five questions to ask my CISO, trades and functions*

Regulations

4.1. The context

Fifty years ago, we would not have accepted that our mail should be opened, but an email can be considered a postcard sent without an envelope. We would have reacted strongly if our movements had been known, our expenses tracked, our readings and purchases studied by third parties.

90% of the data produced worldwide have been produced in the last two years.

The main data producers are the digital platforms of companies and connected objects: smartphones, pacemakers, elevators, refrigerators or breast pumps.

Personal data (credit cards, social security number, email address, etc.) have a value. Personal data is of interest to companies, the State and hackers. The rapid evolution of the digitization of services and globalization has created a new data-based economy: the more data a company collects about its customers, the more services or products it can offer them.

In return for their personal information, given free of charge to site publishers, social networks, taxi or apartment platforms, search engines or online distribution sites, new challenges for the protection of personal data have emerged.

Technologies allow both private companies and public authorities to use personal data. Increasingly, individuals are making information about themselves publicly and globally accessible, most of the time without being aware of the use of such data for commercial, political, social or criminal purposes.

This is a major upheaval in society and global balances: the platforms and providers of digital services and products are mainly American (GAFAM) or Chinese (BATX). In return for the data we have given them, without really knowing what we are giving them, they have the ability to colonize Europe, they know our tastes, consumption and travel habits, our lifestyle and health data, our financial resources, our friends, our interests, our professional background and projects, the hotels in which we stay, the restaurants we frequent, the sites (physical and digital) we visit, the books and newspapers we read, the films we watch.

4.1.1. *Complaints filed with the CNIL*

The number of complaints filed with the CNIL, which is responsible for ensuring the proper use of personal data, increased by more than 32% in 2018, mainly due to the entry into force of the European Data Protection Regulation (GDPR) in May 2018: the *Commission nationale de l'informatique et des libertés* registered 11,077 complaints in 2018, compared with 8,300 in 2017.

Of the 310 controls carried out in 2018, 49 resulted in a formal notice. For example, we saw insurance companies and companies specializing in advertising targeting via mobile applications among the first sectors targeted: 11 sanctions were imposed, including 10 financial penalties, 7 of which concerned breaches of personal data security. Uber, Bouygues Telecom, Dailymotion and Optical Center are among the companies sanctioned.

More than a third (35.7%) of the complaints received concerned the dissemination of data on the Internet, with a request to delete such data, whether identity data, accounts, photos or videos.

Trade and marketing is the second most complaining sector, accounting for 21% of the total, with in particular a "very sharp increase in complaints concerning SMS prospecting", which is most often done without prior consent.

Among the other sectors concerned, human resources, in particular excessive video surveillance or geolocation, are the subject of 16.5% of complaints.

As stated in the CNIL's 2018 activity report, "citizens aspire to see their personal data collected and used in a transparent manner and for uses they accept. Companies must strive to experience regulation as a requirement that can provide them with a distinctive competitive advantage" and increased stakeholder confidence.

Europe has decided to protect its citizens with the GDPR, and companies must comply therewith, protect the personal data they collect and secure their information systems.

4.1.2. *Vectaury*

Vectaury operates in retail analytics, i.e. the analysis of customer data for the distribution sector. Founded in October 2014, Vectaury employs approximately 70 people and claims to work with more than 100 brands and agencies.

The start-up has created a geolocation cookie that you install on your smartphone without realizing it when you download certain applications, such as games and services such as weather or certain media.

The data collected is then cross-referenced and analyzed so that Vectaury's customers (store chains such as Carrefour) display targeted advertising on people's terminals from the places they have visited.

Start-ups like Vectaury directly negotiate with application distributors to integrate their cookies into the application, as a package that comes with the service.

The user receives a short message informing him/her of the presence of cookies for advertising targeting or marketing purposes, and must give his/her consent.

For the CNIL, accepting the presence of cookies by downloading an application is not enough. When a user downloads an application containing the cookie of Vectaury, it should therefore be informed and allow the continuous tracking of its geolocation data (even when the application is closed) for advertising purposes.

For the CNIL, consent is "not validly collected"; the institution states that Vectaury has thus collected "more than 42 million advertising identifiers and geolocation data from more than 32,000 applications". As the data collected reveal the movements of people and therefore their lifestyle, Vectaury has three months to implement consent requests in accordance with the GDPR and delete the data it had improperly collected. Otherwise, the CNIL may impose a sanction. Indeed, non-compliance with European law (GDPR) leads to a significant risk of sanction: a fine of up to 4% of annual worldwide turnover or €20 million.

Compliance with corporate regulations and rules is a condition of trust for shareholders, rating agencies, directors, auditors and all stakeholders – customers, suppliers, employees, etc.

4.1.3. *Optical Center*

In July 2017, the CNIL was informed of a "significant data leak" concerning the company Optical Center.

By entering several URLs in a browser's address bar, it was possible to access hundreds of invoices from the company's customers. These invoices contained data such as surname, first name, postal address and health data (ophthalmological correction) or, in some cases, the social security number of the persons concerned.

The www.optical-center.fr website had a security breach, which had already been reported in 2015. It did not include a feature to verify that a customer is properly connected to his/her personal space ("customer space") before displaying his/her invoices.

The CNIL imposed a financial penalty of 250,000 euros and decided to make its decision public.

4.1.4. *Dailymotion*

In December 2016, a press article reported a major data leak related to the Dailymotion platform, which indicated that the data breach was the result of a multi-step attack involving 82.5 million email addresses and 18.3 million encrypted passwords.

The attackers were able to access the credentials of an administrator account in the company's database, stored in plain text on the collaborative development platform "GitHub". The attackers then exploited a vulnerability found in the code of the Dailymotion platform on "GitHub". This vulnerability allowed them to use the administrator account to remotely access the company's database and extract users' personal data.

The CNIL imposed a financial penalty of 50,000 euros, considering that the company had failed to comply with its obligation to protect personal data. The company should not have stored identifiers for an administrator account in its source code in plain text; since people outside the company had to remotely connect to the internal computer network, it should have framed these connections by an IP address filtering system or a virtual private network (VPN).

4.2. The different international regulations (data protection)

Worldwide, data protection legislation (sometimes referred to as data confidentiality in third countries) is developing. Legislative texts are often influenced by European Union regulations, which are considered the benchmark for data protection.

More than 100 countries worldwide have data protection legislation, including the 28 member states of the European Union.

While the United States (the State of California is an exception) refuses to protect users and allows Internet service providers to sell their subscribers' personal data (browsing history, geolocation, time spent on an application, etc.) to marketing agencies, other states, including China, are taking the European lead, in order to protect citizens or residents, and make companies that process their personal data accountable.

The State of California in the United States, Brazil, India and Canada have their own regulations. Recent data misuse scandals are accelerating this trend. So, there is a global awareness.

4.2.1. *The United States*

Unlike European law, American regulation is organized by sector of activity or category of individuals: financial services, health sectors, credit institutions, insurance have specific regulations, Fair and Accurate Credit Transactions Act, Health Insurance Portability and Accountability. For individuals, one regulation specifically concerns children: Children's Online Privacy Protection restricts the use of information collected from children under 13 years of age by websites.

In addition, the Clarifying Lawful Overseas Use of Data Act (CLOUD Act) is a US federal law passed on March 23, 2018, on the monitoring of personal data, including in the cloud. It allows law enforcement agencies (federal or local, including municipal) to obtain an individual's personal data without the individual being informed, nor their country of residence, nor the country where the data are stored.

The CLOUD Act makes it legal to capture any email or other digital data stored on US servers, including those abroad. Major local cloud players and their subsidiaries must comply with it, as well as foreign companies operating in the United States.

If a company wants to equip itself with a highly secure solution to manage its data, the choice of a cloud service provider is therefore essential.

4.2.2. *China*

China's first major laws on cybersecurity and personal data protection were introduced in 2012.

The law adopted in 2016 prohibits the sale of personal data of service users "without the consent of the person whose information has been collected", and companies, as in Europe, can only collect data necessary for the services they provide.

As in the United States, and unlike Europe and many countries, China has a sectoral approach to data protection. Many provisions deal with system security, system control and data transfers abroad. With regard to data protection, the regulations apply to network operators.

China is also very restrictive with regard to the Internet. Indeed, Internet service providers are controlled by the government, which has legislated to be able to block the content of certain sites, monitor Internet access for people in China, residents and foreigners. Baidu, Tencent and Alibaba, which are among the largest companies in the field in the world, are benefiting from the blocking of international competitors, particularly American, on the Chinese market. China blocked access to Wikipedia in 2019.

4.2.3. *Asia*

In South Korea and Japan, as in other Asian countries, Hong Kong, Taiwan, the Philippines or Singapore, progress is also very rapid and in the direction of European law, even if the notion of personal data is a little different. India is also inspired by European law.

4.2.4. *Europe*

In Europe, the new European Data Protection Regulation (GDPR), described in more detail below, entered into force on May 25, 2018, throughout the European Union (EU). In some cases, it may also apply to companies based outside the EU. Swiss companies, for example, will have to comply with the GDPR if they process the personal data of individuals resident in the EU territory and if the processing activities are linked to an offer of goods or services to these individuals (with or without payment) or to monitoring the behavior of these individuals.

4.3. Cybersecurity regulations, the NIS Directive

The European directive NIS (Security of Network and Information Systems) aims to considerably strengthen the resilience of digital Europe, by setting up cooperation between States, monitoring centers and "digital fire brigades".

As with physical security, if investors, companies and individuals cannot trust infrastructure, administrations, services and products, how can they be attracted to Europe?

Digital trust is a major asset for the economy.

The NIS Directive concerns all actors and in particular "essential service operators", such as certain actors in the energy, transport, banking, financial market infrastructure, health, drinking water supply and distribution sectors, as well as "digital service providers".

Essential service operators as well as online marketplaces, search engines and cloud services will therefore be subject to new security and incident reporting requirements. The main objective is to ensure a high level of security of networks and information systems common to the whole EU.

The NIS Cybersecurity Directive requires a wide range of private sector companies to comply with new security and incident notifications. It also stipulates that "critical infrastructure operators", i.e. public utilities, transport and financial service companies, must deploy appropriate measures to manage security risks and report serious incidents to a national authority or to the emergency IT response team.

4.4. Sectoral regulations

4.4.1. *The banking industry*

In addition to the NIS Directive, published in 2016, the G7 countries have established a list of fundamental elements of cybersecurity for the financial sector, recommendations on the need to assess cybersecurity and coordination with other critical sectors. The CPMI-IOSCO (Committee on Payments and Market-International Organization of Securities Commissions Infrastructures) published the *Cyber resilience for financial market infrastructures* guide in June 2016.

On June 19, 2017, the ECB organized a high-level meeting on cyber resilience in Frankfurt. In his speech, Benoît Coeuré, a member of the ECB's Executive Board, spoke about the objectives of this meeting with representatives of public authorities, critical service providers and financial market infrastructures.

He stressed the inevitability of the attacks and the absolute need to take action to ensure the resilience of the system as a whole, with each country's system linked to the others. He announced the creation of a High-level Cyber Resilience Forum, in particular, to ensure that cybersecurity is not only a matter for regulators but also tp:

– better understand the threat in Europe, particularly the financial sector;

– share the cyber strategy and explain the ECB's approach to addressing the issue of cyber resilience for banks;

– establish cooperation and create an environment of trust.

Indeed, the Basel rules aim to strengthen the stability of banks, but the other source of instability is not financial, it is technological: the whole system is based on digital operation, the risk is systemic and cybersecurity is vital. The ECB therefore has requirements in terms of governance, identification measures, protection measures, detection capabilities, as well as response and recovery solutions after the cyber crisis. Cyber-resilience guides also recommend crisis simulation, communication preparation, continuous improvement and learning

In addition to financial stress tests, on May 2, 2018, the ECB published a European framework for testing the resilience of the financial system to TIBER-EU (Threat Intelligence Based Ethical Red Teaming) cyber-attacks: TIBER-EU-based tests simulate a cyber-attack against an entity's critical functions and underlying systems, such as the people it employs, the processes it implements and the technologies it uses. These tests will help the entity assess its capabilities in terms of protection, detection and response to potential cyber-attacks.

The ECB intervenes in banking institutions either as a preventive measure or following an incident, and most probably visited BNP, where two major breakdowns occurred in two months, in early 2019 (three days of blackout of the information system for the second breakdown), due to a "simple network incident", says BNP. A bank has strict obligations regarding the availability of its service, in line with its status as a critical national infrastructure, no matter the cause of the incidents (hardware or software failure, network failure or computer attack).

"The ECB's banking supervision attaches great importance to cyber resilience", warns Sabine Lautenschläger. The European supervisor thus conducts audits concerning IT risk management, on-site control of the implementation of best practices and has set up a reporting system for IT incidents.

4.4.2. *Health*

Health data are specific personal data because they are considered sensitive.

Interconnection, increased exchanges and data sharing increase security risks: data theft or misuse, system blocking, hacking of connected medical devices, etc.

The appointment schedules of some hospitals were hacked by criminals, who contacted patients to tell them that their consultation was cancelled and gave them a premium number to call to reschedule. Today, scanners, MRIs or incubators for premature babies are connected and can therefore be hacked.

To better understand the increase in the number of attacks, health facilities are required to report all attacks through the Adverse Health Event Reporting Portal. The Ministry of Solidarity and Health, in conjunction with the regional health agencies (ARS) and ASIP Santé, has set up an operational support unit to help them.

The text provides, among other things, for the certification of personal data protection by an accredited body.

The health sector, unlike the banking industry, is not ahead of the curve. And yet, like other sectors, it is extremely dependent on information technology, both for medical interventions, administrative management and the storage of patients' medical records.

Healthcare facility information systems are a perfect target for cybercriminals. The impacts can be both economic and operational: a failure in the operating system can equally endanger patients' lives. The 2017 attack in the United Kingdom caused a complete paralysis of the imaging departments and the opening of patient files from various hospitals.

The problem is serious and increasingly complex: with the development of outpatient and home-based hospitals, institutions are increasingly connected.

Appropriate tools, such as anonymization and blockchain, regular security audits (physical and IT), training of medical personnel, appropriate processes, a budget for data protection and system security are necessary for the compliance of the GDPR by the entire health sector.

4.5. The General Data Protection Regulation (GDPR)

The General Data Protection Regulation (GDPR) unifies existing data protection regulations in EU countries under a single law, introducing guidelines on how companies will have to manage personally identifiable information.

The GDPR has several objectives:

– strengthen the rights of individuals, in particular by improving transparency on the use of their data, the possibility of giving their consent or not to the use of their data and the creation of a right to the portability of personal data;

– make accountable the employees processing the personal data (data controllers and subcontractors);

– develop cooperation between data protection authorities, which may in particular adopt joint decisions (in particular on sanctions) when data processing operations are transnational.

The GDPR, as explained below, therefore allows the consumer to become aware of the use of his or her personal data, to give consent or to refuse to allow his or her data to be used for a particular purpose.

Companies must ensure that they have appropriate security solutions, procedures and policies in place, at the risk of incurring severe penalties for non-compliance, up to €20 million or, in the case of a company, 4% of the previous year's total worldwide turnover (whichever is higher).

The amount of the fines will vary according to the nature, gravity and duration of the violation and taking into account the scope or purpose of the processing operation concerned, as well as the number of persons affected and the level of damage they have suffered. The degree of responsibility of the controller or processor is also taken into account, as well as the various technical and organizational measures already in place to ensure the company's compliance.

The GDPR introduces the notion of the responsibility of economic actors at the highest level of the company and its organization, in data governance, IT risk management and the prevention of massive data leaks.

For companies, it is a question of compliance, a financial issue (fine, loss of customers) and a question of digital trust (reputation damaged in the event of a data leak).

4.5.1. *The foundations*

The foundations are as follows:

– the strengthening of individuals' rights: it requires the collection and retention of consent to the processing of personal data;

– the obligation to inform: it requires structures that are victims of hacking of personal data to inform the CNIL and the data subjects whose information has been stolen within 72 hours;

– heavy sanctions: it sets up dissuasive sanctions, up to €20 million or 4% of an organization's worldwide turnover. The higher amount is the one retained;

– the principle of minimization of the data collected: it requires only the information strictly necessary for the purposes for which it is processed to be collected;

– the right of data portability: persons whose information has been collected have the right to request to receive personal data concerning them;

– the data register: it obliges organizations to track all personal data processing operations carried out within the organization.

4.5.2. *Definition of personal data*

Different categories of data need to be distinguished:

– personal data: name, first name, email, telephone, pseudonym, IP address, fingerprints;

– financial data: GNI, salary, transactions, consumption patterns, opinion, policy or union data;

– health-related data: medical records, sick leave, care, weight, sports activity, eating habits, etc.;

– data relating to computer habits: Internet browsing, social networks, interests, contacts, photos, etc.;

– context data: geolocation, movements, Wi-Fi connections.

4.5.3. *The so-called "sensitive" data*

Sensitive data require enhanced measures that are required under the GDPR (impact analysis, enhanced information, consent gathering, etc.). This is the information:

– revealing alleged racial or ethnic origin;

– relating to political, philosophical or religious opinions;

– relating to trade union membership;

– concerning health or sexual orientation;

– genetic or biometric;

– data on offenses or criminal convictions.

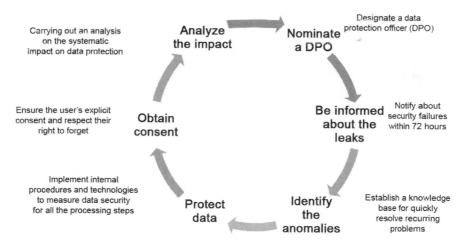

Figure 4.1. *Complying with the GDPR (source: Starboard Advisory). For a color version of this figure, see www.iste.co.uk/defreminville/cybersecurity.zip*

4.5.4. *The principles of the GDPR*

4.5.4.1. *Transparency*

The company must therefore be precisely aware of the uses it has of the data because it must be transparent by reworking, in particular, its communication and be able to respond to people's requests for rights.

4.5.4.2. *Minimization*

The company must ensure that the data collection does not go beyond what is strictly necessary for the purpose set for your use. Any data not useful for processing and not justified should therefore not be collected (or deleted if already recovered).

4.5.4.3. *Data security*

It is necessary to strengthen the means to ensure proper data protection through technical and organizational measures.

It is mandatory to structure the data security process as soon as a new processing operation is designed.

In the event of a leak of personal data likely to create a risk for rights and freedoms, you must notify this violation to the ICO within 72 hours.

4.5.4.4. *Accountability*

The company must demonstrate that it is aware of the requirements of the new regulations and that it has:

– sensitized its employees;

– initiated a voluntary compliance process;

– implemented the duties and obligations for data processing and in particular high-risk processing;

– established a time-bound action plan to achieve full compliance.

4.5.5. *The five actions to be in compliance with the GDPR*

Compliance with the GDPR is achieved through:

– mapping company data: knowing what data is collected, where the data is processed and stored;

– data protection: restrict access to authorized users for legitimate tasks;

– access control, which is the essential corollary of the previous point;

– logging of operations, in order to be able to prove good faith;

– data destruction: destroyed data is data that cannot be stolen from you.

4.5.6. *The processing register*

As the cornerstone of compliance (starting point, monitoring tool, or even proof of compliance on certain aspects), the register may be required by customers and supervisory authorities.

The questions to be answered by the processing register are as follows:

– Why: what is the purpose of the processing?

– Who: who is responsible for the processing?

– What: which data are concerned and who are concerned?

– Where: where are the data hosted?

– How long: until when are the data stored?

– How: how is the data stored, and what are the security measures?

4.5.7. *The five actions to be carried out*

4.5.7.1. *Appointment of a DPO*

The DPO (Data Protection Officer), in charge of compliance, is the contact point for the authorities. This is mandatory for a company with 250 or more employees. This role does not necessarily correspond to a new position in the company. It can be entrusted to the IT or CIO manager, a legal manager or a qualified person outside the company.

Responsible for internal compliance monitoring, advice on data protection obligations and the relationship with supervisory authorities and data subjects, the role of the DPO is complex and extensive.

By conducting regular security audits and making recommendations to ensure compliance with regulations and best practices throughout the organization, the DPO also ensures that employees are informed of compliance requirements and that data processing personnel are trained and made aware of them.

4.5.7.2. *Compliance plan*

This action plan corresponds to the implementation of data governance within the company:

– Organization: who are the persons responsible for the collection, processing of data, access management, and protection and security?

– Documentation: how are the purposes of the processing operations and the content of the operations documented?

– Alignment of processes: what are the processes across the company?

– Training/communication: who is responsible for the training? What is the training plan? When will the training take place?

This action plan must be defined with the various managers of the company (the team will depend on the size of the company and its type of activity): the DPO, human resources, the sales and marketing department, the IT manager and the IT security manager.

It is not enough to know the GDPR; it is essential to understand the environment, activities, data required for operations, as well as the legal constraints, IT systems and procedures of the company.

It is also important to be able to communicate internally and externally and to be able to define and implement procedures relating, for example, to the right to forget or the right to data portability.

Compliance with the GDPR requires the involvement of all company functions: IT, marketing, human resources and most other departments of the company.

4.5.7.3. *Produce/update the processing of personal data*

The company, the DPO and its various functions/operations must verify and communicate the purpose for which they collect user data, the nature of the data (personal, sensitive, etc.) and the duration of their retention.

Collection is increasingly digital and stored digitally. It can also be done by phone and then stored digitally.

Once the data has been mapped, the location of the storage and the media, as well as the subcontractors involved, must be identified.

4.5.7.4. *Update websites/documents*

Websites and applications must be updated with the new legal notices and an explicit management of consent with a reminder of the purpose of the processing operation, not to mention the option of opposition and unsubscription.

4.5.7.5. *Write to subcontractors and partners affected*

The company must take care of the software publishers, data hosts and IT service providers with whom it works and ensure that the steps are taken in accordance with the law.

One of the complexities of the DPO's role, beyond compliance with the GDPR, is to assess the company's compliance with its commitments.

Indeed, it is one thing to ask customers to consent (or not) to the collection, storage and use of their personal data by the company or third parties with a clear purpose; it is another to check whether the company respects the customer's wishes.

For example:

– if the customer refuses, does the DPO ensure that the company does not collect and store its data?

– if the customer refuses third-party cookies, is the DPO able to ensure that third parties do not have access to the personal information of customers who connect to the company's website?

– if subsidiaries or suppliers (e.g. delivery companies) collect customer information, what happens to this information once the customer is served and delivered? Is access to this information secure? Do contracts with suppliers allow the company to audit the quality of the systems and procedures of its suppliers, partners or uncontrolled subsidiaries (if they are joint ventures)?

Moreover, it is one thing to ask site or application publishers to comply with the GDPR and another thing to verify that third parties, such as advertising agencies, are well informed of the consent or refusal of customers and the respect of this response.

4.5.8. Cookies

Cookies allow you to know which computer, tablet or smartphone is viewing which content on the Internet. Traces of website visitors, especially when combined with other information received by servers, can be used to create profiles of individuals and to identify them.

Web browsing data can then be used to create high-performance targeted and/or personalized advertising and to establish profiles of consumers or professionals according to their areas of interest in order to offer them profiled commercial offers that are almost "tailor-made".

In accordance with the GDPR, profiling is not prohibited; it must only be the subject of prior information to the profiled person and a special mention of the right of objection (Article 21.2 GDPR). The Internet user must be clearly informed and have the opportunity to say no to the use of his/her data.

Some "technical" cookies help to improve navigation on a website. Others allow website publishers to identify users and then send them advertising. Advertisers may also sometimes place cookies on the site. It is therefore essential for the company to monitor the activity of third parties (advertising boards and advertisers) who place themselves with or without the company's agreement between the website and site visitors, to contractually formalize relations with site publishers and to include in these contracts the authorized links between site publishers and advertisers.

Is the agreement of these visitors respected and are the company's commitments to its customers respected? Tools (cookie trackers) are developed for the management of customer agreements and also for the activity of third parties, in order to verify that they are authorized by the company and the customer and that contractual relationships are adapted and respected, both financially and operationally.

4.6. Consequences for the company and the board of directors

It is essential for directors and officers to be aware of consumer trends and purchasing criteria. Indeed, according to the Internet Society and Consumers International study conducted in March 2019, among 6,381 people in France, the United Kingdom, the United States, Canada and Australia, consumers were concerned about their privacy and personal data in the face of the intrusion of these potential snitches that are multiplying within the home. Eighty-eight percent of the adults surveyed want governments to set up a "legal framework", "dedicated to security and privacy for connected objects". Sixty percent of them state that "the existence of a label or information specifying the guarantee of data security compliance has an influence on the purchasing act". Seventy-three percent of French people "are afraid that their data will be used without their prior consent".

Eighty-three percent of the French respondents believe that manufacturers must guarantee data confidentiality and user safety by "exclusively offering" products that preserve these values. Manufacturers, at least some of them, have understood these concerns well.

In addition, besides commercial issues, an action plan for compliance must be put in place: organization, documentation, alignment of processing operations, training/communication, name of the person in charge, date of commissioning. This action plan will be defined depending on the company and its activity with the CIO, the business lines, HR and customer management.

In particular, it will be necessary to:

– produce/update the processing of personal data: purpose, users, responsible, nature, retention period;

– map the data, identify the location of the storage, the media and the subcontractors involved;

– update websites and documents with the new legal notices and explicit management of consent with a reminder of the purpose of the processing operation, not to mention the option of opposition;

– involve subcontractors and partners affected: software publishers, data hosts, IT service providers.

In the event of criminal proceedings, the managers may be held liable if it is shown that they were negligent or that they were personally at fault. The offenses concerned are invasion of privacy, non-compliance with formalities (request for consent), processing of sensitive data when it has not been authorized, failure to communicate security breaches to IT service providers, collection of personal data by fraudulent means and retention of sensitive data without consent.

– What are the company's values regarding customer data?

– What is your knowledge of the real situation: data collected, data processing, organization and processes?

– Do you know which third parties hold the data/collect your customers' data? Do you know where the company's data is stored and under what conditions?

– Have you assessed the risks of non-compliance (internally or through an independent audit)?

– In which countries does the company operate and to which legislation is it subject?

Box 4.1. *The five points of vigilance regarding data protection*

5

Best Practices of the Board of Directors

The responses to be provided are multiple: individual and collective, educational, technical, legal and regulatory.

Many pitfalls are to be avoided:

– you have a CISO, everything is fine;

– cybersecurity is an IT problem;

– the tools (antivirus, firewall, SOC and CERT) are in place;

– the company is too small to be attacked;

– BYOD (Bring Your Own Device) policy is "safe";

– the threats come only from the outside;

– the company is 100% secure, no need for audit or testing;

– our data is in the cloud, everything is fine;

– our data has no value;

– our service providers are responsible;

– industrial infrastructure is not concerned;

– we have nothing to hide.

5.1. Digital skills

Although many corporate directors consider cybersecurity to be an operational issue, the liability of the board of directors may be sought in the event of negligence or mismanagement, if the sustainability of the company is at risk, as a result of cybersecurity issues, lack of risk management and internal control.

"The composition of the board of directors must be adapted to the company's challenges", says APIA (*Association professionnelle des administrateurs indépendants*). "The diversity of the Board's members must therefore be analyzed in the light of their skills and experience, particularly in the face of digital challenges".

This digital competence is necessary both for strategic issues, for the assessment of cyber-risks and also for the assessment of the executive management's digital skills, its ability to change the internal organization, its customer relations, the production tool and the company's culture (digital natives aspire to a faster, more transparent and more collaborative organization than the generations in power cannot ignore).

Administrators do not need to be digital experts to exercise their responsibilities and understand strategy and risk through a digital lens. Their understanding of the issues, their network, and their ability to interact with the company's experts, internal or external auditors, and risk managers are now essential for all companies and organizations.

When this issue of the digital skills of the boards of directors is raised in director circles, the answers are edifying:

– administrators do not have digital skills;

– it is not a subject that goes back to the board;

– this is an operational issue;

– we do not have time to address these issues; the board's agenda focuses on strategy and financial performance.

The evolution of the boards of directors is far too slow in relation to digital issues. Regulations and new skills found among the boards are the main factors enabling their transformation.

All stakeholders, investors, financial analysts and clients will welcome the appointment of a competent director in this area.

5.2. Situational awareness

A good knowledge of the situation is the first step in the effectiveness of the board of directors and executive management, both in terms of content and speed.

It is therefore necessary to define the information to be shared, the frequency and the means. Digital tools make it possible to reduce the information asymmetry between the board of directors and executive management. Indeed, administrators have direct and real-time access, via the press, Google alerts and social networks, to information about the company, competitors, critical countries or suppliers or main customers.

In addition, the possibility of sharing certain data in real time with executive management should facilitate exchanges between directors and officers, even if it is necessary to remain attentive to the responsibilities of each and every one and to the importance for the board of directors to maintain a certain distance from daily life (except in the event of a crisis) and to keep an eye on the long-term course.

5.2.1. *The main issues*

In 2018, the United States Securities and Exchange Commission (SEC) issued guidance for listed companies on cybersecurity disclosures. As cyber incidents are increasingly making the headlines, companies and regulators recognize that cyber incidents are not a passing trend, but rather a risk inherent in our new and sustainable economy. The SEC's view of the role of the board of directors has evolved in recent years and resulted in the publication of the 2018 guidance document. Corporate directors are now expected to get involved and, therefore, must demand greater visibility for what is often presented as a dark and very complex area that is best left to technologists. Even if this document is not very specific about the actions to be taken (these are specific to each company), some recommendations can be identified.

5.2.1.1. *It starts with the CEO! –tone from the top*

If the chief executive officer does not understand the importance of cybersecurity, the board will have difficulty exercising its responsibilities and ensuring that appropriate risk-based measures are in place and functioning. The risk is often minimized, and managers may become aware of the potential impacts when the damage has already been done. The consequences can be immediate and sometimes catastrophic.

Therefore, boards of directors must take proactive steps to ensure that the chief executive officer makes cybersecurity preparedness an organizational priority. Without the leadership and day-to-day objectives given by the CEO, any cybersecurity program is likely to fail. The actions of the board of directors or their absence will also be examined.

5.2.1.2. *Avoiding the method of checking checklists of checkpoints*

It is certainly not the task of the board of directors to be responsible for the day-to-day implementation of the company's cybersecurity program. But the board of directors must be involved, use available resources, understand and evaluate the adequacy of the measures taken and require active and continuous visibility.

In cybersecurity, as with other topics, "ticking the box" can help create a false sense of trust. The key questions for the boards are: does the company have a cybersecurity program in place? Is this program effective? To assess these questions, board members must look beyond the surface and seek to understand whether the policies and procedures in place are truly adapted to meet the organization's unique needs.

Boards of directors must determine whether the company's management team does not consider cybersecurity to be a problem that is primarily addressed by the IT department.

5.2.1.3. *Assigning clear supervisory responsibilities at the board level*

According to the 2018 guidelines, the company must include – in its disclosures – a description of how the board of directors manages its risk oversight function. As with other audit and risk issues, the board could logically assign this oversight to its existing audit or risk committee.

However, in some particularly sensitive companies, it is recommended that a new board committee be appointed to deal exclusively with cybersecurity issues: cyber insurance, incident response plans, business continuity plans, internal threats and "bad exits" (those who leave a company and pose a threat, for example by disrupting technological systems), due diligence in the field of third-party cybersecurity; prevention and response against ransomware; recruitment of IT staff; training in cybersecurity; data security budget, etc.

If a board does not have an expert in cybersecurity, it should consider using an external expert, just as the review of the accounts is carried out by an independent expert.

5.2.1.4. *Requiring evaluations, tests and reports*

The implementation of independent quarterly or semi-annual reports on the status and health of the company's cybersecurity program, training, staffing, assessments, test results or other third-party comments on the overall state of the company's cybersecurity are essential and will demonstrate how the board of directors fulfills its responsibility to monitor risks in this increasingly important area.

Board oversight of cybersecurity audits should include not only a thorough review of risk and security assessments, penetration test reports and other similar audits related to cybersecurity but also corrective efforts or measures that will be implemented in the future.

Similarly, boards should also ask management to participate in practical exercises that allow organizations to analyze potential emergencies.

Boards must carefully examine the effectiveness, timeliness, frequency and overall results of a company's simulation exercise and, more importantly, analyze the corrective actions taken after these exercises.

5.2.1.5. *Remaining vigilant at all times*

The most recent and efficient solutions are not enough. They must be properly deployed, and a program that integrates employee awareness and training must be incorporated into the cyber device. All employees must be vigilant and encouraged to report perceived problems as they arise. Speed of response is essential and is the key to recovery.

Boards should obtain information on the frequency and effectiveness of IT security training programs: list of trained individuals, including board members, tests (fraudulent email campaigns and test results), data access policy and IT charters.

5.2.1.6. *Being informed and understanding incidents*

The ability to detect and respond to a cyber incident is essential and can be critical to the results. An effective program can position the company for a rapid recovery and isolate it from reputation damage.

On the other hand, a failed program may further exacerbate the underlying incident, exposing the company to significant legal risks and reputation damage. Boards of directors must be immediately informed by the company's management when a serious IT incident has been identified. This will demonstrate that the board is fully involved and takes its governance responsibilities seriously.

SEC Directives 2018 reinforce this notion of alerting the board. SEC President Jay Clayton, who testified before Congress about a data breach suffered by the SEC, clearly deplored that SEC staff did not share some critical information about the data breach.

The board of directors must understand any historical events in cybersecurity that may have affected the company, its competitors or other stakeholders.

5.2.1.7. *Anticipating*

With the publication of its guidelines for 2018, the SEC has issued a call for companies' boards of directors to wake up. The risk of cybersecurity has clearly risen to the top of the corporate agenda and, in reality, boards of directors must now engage in careful and rigorous oversight of the planning and response to cybersecurity incidents.

Given the current landscape of class actions related to cybersecurity issues, data security incidents not only create regulatory liability, but can also create personal liability for administrators.

The priority is to monitor these risks, exactly as for financial risks.

– Is the board informed of past cyber-attacks and their severity? Is it sure to be warned in case of an attack?

– When were the last intrusion tests or an independent external audit carried out? What were the results?

– According to management, what is the most serious cyber vulnerability: IT systems, tools, personnel or processes?

– Does the company have security policies and procedures? Are they tested and audited?

– What are the company's cyber-risks, are cyber-risks integrated into the company's risk management system, and what are the priorities?

Box 5.1. *Five questions for the board of directors*

5.2.2. *Insurance*

As mentioned above, updating the insurance contract will make it possible to check the quality of the protection system, security policies and potential vulnerabilities.

There are many guides that can be consulted by companies, especially SMEs, which often do not have an IT security expert, or subsidiaries of international groups, which are not always on the radar of their parent company.

These guides will make it possible to carry out a self-assessment, an essential prerequisite for consulting a broker or an insurance company, which will refuse to insure a company that has not done the minimum in terms of cybersecurity.

The insurance approach is virtuous; it makes it possible to carry out an assessment of the company's security by answering the insurance company's questionnaire, sometimes with the support of the insurance broker. If the insurance company refuses to implement a cyber extension of your contract, worry.

The guide of the FFA (*Fédération française de l'assurance*) is recommended by the government and ANSSI. It gives many practical recommendations.

5.3. Internal governance

5.3.1. *The CISO*

It is not enough to have found the rare pearl: an excellent CISO. The latter must interact with the business and support functions and be "connected" to the executive committee and the board of directors.

He/she is the contact person for the executive committee and the board of directors, sometimes via the audit and risk committee, and informs them of the company's exposure to risks, incidents and the measures to be implemented.

It is essential that the CISO is well informed about projects and involved with operational and functional departments (e.g. purchasing, mergers and acquisitions), in order to be able to provide a transversal vision, adjust strategies and action plans, after having measured the effectiveness of the measures.

He or she relies on a CISO channel within the company (branches, subsidiaries), establishes the security policy applicable within the group, disseminates it and ensures that it is applied in conjunction with the internal audit department. It is important that the CISO has a list of correspondents in all the controlled legal entities of the group, in order to be able to communicate security policies, enforce them and be informed in the event of an incident.

In the case of joint ventures or consortia, it is important to define when setting up these entities, within the shareholders' agreements, which security policies will apply, who will be able to audit their application, and who will appoint the CIO and the CISO. The persons in charge of negotiating shareholder agreements should be made aware of these aspects.

Some companies have integrated the director of cybersecurity into the executive committee, just as other companies have created a digital committee on the board of directors.

Its scope is broad, since it deals with all information systems: industrial, management, commercial, as well as site protection, and extended enterprise protection, with suppliers, subcontractors, service providers and subsidiaries in all the countries where the group has deployed activities. SMEs, which do not escape digitization, do not always have sufficient resources to ensure the security of their operations: there are "cyberdeaths" among these companies.

The cybersecurity manager is an essential link in the chain, but their effectiveness and performance depend on the organization as a whole and on their interaction with the company's main internal and external stakeholders.

Their missions are multiple and are part of the objective of developing and maintaining the digital trust that stakeholders (customers, suppliers, employees, shareholders, partners, etc.) have in the company, its products and services: finding trusted partners, ensuring the company's resilience with limited resources and budgets. Protecting strategic and personal data is a challenge for cybersecurity managers in a context of cost reduction, automation and optimization.

It is necessary to know how to protect strategic, financial and personal information, as well as how to intervene from the design stage (Privacy & Security by Design), to advise the business in the development of applications and services that make it possible to develop digital activities and create value, by becoming a trusted partner for traditional and new customers, to contribute to compliance, particularly in the context of the GDPR or the NIS directive, to establish the synthesis of cyber-risks by relativizing the various risks: a lack of security in industrial systems can have much more serious consequences for the company than a leak of non-strategic or non-sensitive data.

5.3.2. *The CISO and the company*

In cybersecurity, it is essential that everyone assumes their responsibilities: the board of directors, managers, the IT department, the CISO, as well as the business operations, functions, employees, the extended company (suppliers, subcontractors, IT service providers), not to mention the

State (infrastructures, education, investigations, standards, certifications and regulations).

Managers within the company too often work in silos, while security, physical or digital, is everyone's business and requires a 360-degree panoramic view.

The business must be involved in risk mapping and also in the solutions to be implemented, in the identification of strategic assets and in the definition of security standards, allowing the right balance to be found between security and agility, security and efficiency.

Threats evolve quickly, which requires being agile and responsive. They can be strong and destabilizing. If the main actors of the company are not prepared, and if they have not understood and become aware of the cyber threat, then they will not be able to respond correctly and avoid impacts.

In regards to cybersecurity, what do your employees think?
Basis: group (174 respondents)

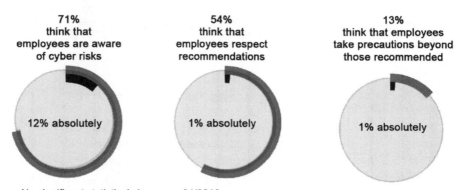

No significant statistical change vs 01/2018

Figure 5.1. *Employees who are aware of cybersecurity, but who are not very involved according to the CISOs (source: according to CESIN)*

"We are all concerned! You have to invest. Lightning can strike anyone. We must anticipate, prevent, and mitigate the effects", Guillaume Poupard regularly insists, particularly on April 17 in front of a packed room at the Institut français des administrateurs (IFA).

Protecting yourself is possible; it requires an effort: you have to start by understanding. And then to respect some major principles, and also, depending on the sector of activity, the regulations. Cybersecurity is not a specialist's business, it must be integrated into all the company's projects.

Internal governance must take into account the safety issues for the company, of course, as well as the issues for the company's functions and the business:

– human resource issues: management involvement in cybersecurity governance and the establishment of a security culture aimed at promoting key people and key skills, all-round training and the development of expertise;

– the financial challenges: allocate more budgets to cybersecurity, measure cyber-risk exposure and make the necessary investments, including the implementation of insurance coverage, collect objective data to assess and manage their cyber performance, compare themselves and decide;

– legal issues: GDPR compliance, as well as the drafting of an IT charter and internal regulations, the management of complaints (those of the company in the event that it is attacked, those of third parties if they have suffered damage and consider the company liable), the development of contracts with suppliers and subcontractors;

– business challenges and business continuity: the security teams, in coordination with the business lines and functions, aim to guarantee safe operation at all times, without compromising either the quality of service or environmental and human protection;

– the quality and safety of suppliers, customers, partners and IT service providers.

The coordination of the various actors (CIO, CISO, DPO, risk manager) with the various business lines of the company (industrial sites, product innovation, sales, support functions), external service providers, users, is a difficulty, but it is a necessity that is the responsibility of the managers, and must be monitored by the board of directors.

The organization and governance of security must be defined precisely and clearly for all: who does what? What are the roles and responsibilities of the CIO, RSI, risk manager, internal audit and external audit? Who is in charge of identifying threats (threat intelligence), monitoring attacks, intervening, defining the security repository, enforcing it, verifying its application? Who depends on whom? What are the reporting lines? What are the degrees of independence of the supervisory bodies?

It is recommended to place the CISO where he/she will have the means to act effectively and where his/her independence will be ensured. The following three principles must be applied for this safety manager:

– a clear mandate;

– proximity to the executive committee;

– freedom of action (and therefore of budget).

It is not recommended that the CISO should be dependent on the IT director whose objective is to make information systems easy to use, fast and efficient. Rather, security measures tend to slow down access to workstations (password, double authentication), applications (passwords, updates) and computer processing.

The internal organization must be global and not ignore entire parts of the company that are sometimes forgotten. The points of vigilance of the internal organization are in particular the following:

– information systems, throughout the company: cyber protection architecture (isolating the various information systems, isolating the company and the industrial network, using inspection and intrusion detection tools), server location, back-up of sensitive data, etc.;

– factories: hardware and software, network access, data access with authentication and authorization plus encryption, physical and digital security coordination, updates, USB sticks, augmented reality tools;

– administrators (tools and access rights rules), users (passwords, mobility, how to communicate, data archiving – how long, where, classification? – back-ups), certified NCSC (National Cyber Security Centre) or NCCIC (National Cybersecurity and Communications Integration Center) service providers;

– decision-making processes and delegations of authority: who makes decisions in terms of tools, product design, access to information, recruitment, procedures (password renewal), choice of service providers and contracts?

Be careful, there is strong pressure on CISOs, who are too often considered responsible in the event of a successful attack. Between the explosion of threats they face, the cyber-risks to be managed internally due to employees with poor IT hygiene or the hammer of the GDPR, the pressure is high.

Indeed, as shown by a study conducted by Symantec on a European scale in collaboration with the University of London and the consulting firm Thread, 82% of security managers in Europe are on the verge of burn-out, a little more in France (85%) than elsewhere (81% in the United Kingdom and Germany). Eight percent plan to resign versus 64% in Germany and 60% in the United Kingdom.

Many alerts to process, the obligation to secure excessive volumes of incoming/outgoing data and too vast an area to protect along with a lack of resources are the main causes of this unease. CISOs must assess risks, propose solutions and decide, due to the lack of involvement of decision makers. CISOs are business partners, not decision makers.

5.3.3. *Clarifying responsibilities*

The companies under attack regularly raise cybersecurity issues at the executive committee and board level: incidents, devices, risks and crisis management.

This is proof that this new challenge is at the level of leaders, not just security managers. Too often, responsibilities lie with the latter, who are responsible for estimating risks, proposing solutions, choosing them and implementing them. That is a lot for one person; the company is in danger. The CISO who described this all too common situation is also in a company that encountered serious problems in the first quarter of 2019.

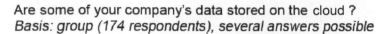

Are some of your company's data stored on the cloud ?
Basis: group (174 respondents), several answers possible

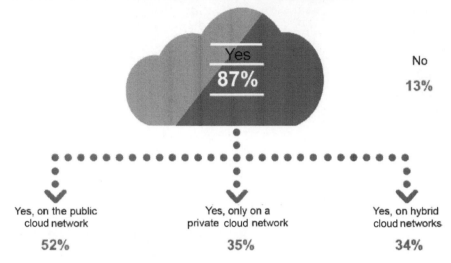

No significant statistical change vs 01/2018

Figure 5.2. *Most companies store at least some of their data in a cloud... most of them in public clouds (source: after CESIN)*

Cybersecurity is a decision maker's subject. We must be able to make trade-offs. We have to talk about it in the executive committee. And talk about it in an understandable way. What is needed is to make informed decisions with legal, commercial, technical and financial officials. Cybersecurity represents 5–10% of the overall IT budget, all inclusive. It is a risk like any other, and risk must be integrated into risk mapping, and the risk analysis must be renewed. The Ebios Risk Manager method has been developed to assess risks using a cyber prism.

A member of the executive committee must be in charge of security matters and will be the referent of the cybersecurity manager. The latter cannot depend on the IT or digital director, who is required to be agile, innovative and efficient. Safety is often a constraint: it slows down and costs money.

Convergence between digital transformation and security is essential. They must move forward together. This is why it is important to talk about the two subjects together from the outset and avoid the temptation of "it was better before".

The cloud *is* complicated for CISOs, but it is necessary to deal with in a secure way to analyze the services of cloud partners.

The identification of outsourced data and services in the cloud cannot be outsourced. It is like strategy.

5.3.4. *Streamlining the supplier portfolio*

In 2018, 54% of IT security managers worked with 10 or fewer solution providers. They are 63% now.

According to the American network equipment manufacturer Cisco and its 2019 report on CISO[1] activity, the trend would be to simplify IT security systems, which are too complex and diversified to be effective and efficient.

The survey was conducted with 3,259 CISOs and CIOs in 18 countries, including France. Seventy-nine percent of respondents still find it difficult, if not very complicated, to orchestrate alerts from multiple suppliers. This is the main reason why more CISOs are now concerned about the reduction of the number of their suppliers, in order to better manage third-party risks and optimize costs.

Also, 51% of respondents estimate the financial impact of a security breach on their organization to be less than $500,000. On the other hand, it would be higher than this amount for 45% of respondents.

The "non-integrated" solutions are too diverse and undermine the process of prioritizing, managing and responding to security alerts.

In addition, 75% also rely on automation to manage IT security priorities, a rate down eight points from 2018. Dependence on disruptive technologies has also declined. Thus, 67% (compared to 77% in 2018) say they use

1 Source: CISO Benchmark Study 2019.

machine learning. In addition, 66% (74% in 2018) report using other artificial intelligence (AI) applications.

Among the following protective solutions, which have been implemented in your company, in addition to antivirus software and a firewall? *Basis: group (174 respondents)/several answers possible*

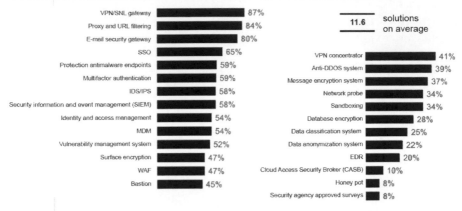

Figure 5.3. *Companies deploy more than a dozen cybersecurity solutions on average (source: according to Cesin)*

5.3.5. *Security policies and procedures*

An employee who inadvertently opens an attachment containing a virus is the primary cause of attacks. The first weapons of defense are internal information and the implementation of procedures.

The attacks are becoming increasingly sophisticated. Surveillance is essential. It is based on tools and everyone's vigilance: setting up a hotline and a dedicated team, communicating to all users about their role to play (detect, question before acting and inform).

The training of all users at all levels (lead by example) is essential: the reminder of rules, good practices and processes (examples: fraud on the president, monitoring processes even in emergencies, checking the origin of instructions).

The existence of an IT security policy and procedures within the company is a good sign. Nevertheless, it is important to update them regularly, especially in the rapidly changing IT field.

In addition, policy coherence must be ensured across the group: for historical reasons, this is not always the case.

Finally, the existence of the security policy is not enough; it must be disseminated to all concerned, including small subsidiaries, and its implementation must be monitored, which means auditing it regularly and monitoring the implementation of recommendations.

The security policy is based on the recipients:

– the IT charter for users with the rules to be respected (Internet, emails, passwords, social media, confidentiality, data management, mobility, authentication);

– the information systems and network security policy;

– security policies, relating to equipment: personal computers (PCs), printers, servers, Wi-Fi, network, telephone;

– security policies toward suppliers and subcontractors;

– back-up policies.

5.3.5.1. *The cloud strategy*

While the cloud has become the central architecture of today's IT, it has also been considered one of the main vulnerabilities, particularly since the United States adopted the CLOUD Act (March 2018).

Internal private cloud, cloud management and outsourced private cloud are becoming increasingly important and provide access to advanced security technologies.

The choice of these solutions is structuring, but the choice of the technical solution (interoperability with the company's systems) is far from sufficient. A risk analysis must also be conducted (such as Ebios or Enisa, as mentioned above).

These are also questions:

– Strategic: what data will be stored on this cloud? What processing will go through the cloud? What back-ups? What availability, reversibility/portability?

– Legal: which contract, which guarantees? Does the service provider comply with the regulations in force? Does the company have the right to audit? Where are the data located? What guarantees of security and confidentiality?

– Financial: annual costs, cost of specific services.

The main measures taken to strengthen data security in the cloud are:

– identification and classification of data, before migrating them;

– the choice of the cloud provider;

– data encryption;

– monitoring user activity around this data;

– the reinforcement of safety rules;

– employee training;

– the classification of data must be done with decision makers and cannot be the sole responsibility of the CIO or CISO. Businesses must understand the issues, data risks and alternative solutions.

5.3.5.2. *The bring your own device (BYOD) strategy*

Teleworking, co-working and the emergence of new BYOD-type uses are forcing companies to develop new ways of working and new tools and therefore to adjust their security systems.

New protection solutions must be deployed, and employees must be made aware of good practices and trained in new tools.

This is a real challenge for companies. It is essential to impose limits: prevent access to certain sites, prohibit the transfer of business documents to personal addresses, and secure outside access to the company's applications and information system. At the same time, if the rules are very cumbersome and complex, employees complain about too many constraints. It is therefore necessary to maintain flexibility and, in this case, to train users so that they know, for example, how to identify malicious emails, identify sites that present risks and avoid connections to unsecured Wi-Fi networks.

In the extreme, some companies could be inspired by companies operating in the military sector, whose computers and industrial sites are not connected to the Internet.

5.3.6. *The human being*

Would you allow AI to make security decisions, concerning detection and/or support? *Basis: group (174 respondents)*

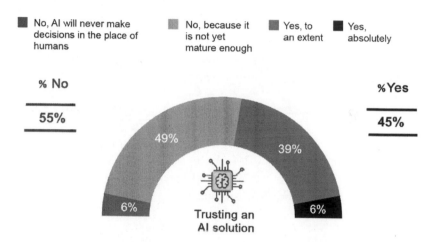

Figure 5.4. *Human intervention remains necessary in the eyes of CISOs (source: according to CESIN). For a color version of this figure, see www.iste.co.uk/defreminville/cybersecurity.zip*

The strong link is the human being, who can also be the weak link: all must be formed, from top to bottom, and from bottom to top. It is therefore necessary to launch an annual training campaign and the latter must be educational: explain the threats and constraints, demand compliance with the rules (crack down if necessary) and involve the entire company.

The commitment of all teams is the best way to reduce the internal threat. This is a real challenge for large companies with complex organizations, where 75% of employees are not aware of the strategy. The loss of meaning and lack of commitment have a direct impact on everyone's vigilance to protect the company.

As mentioned several times, organization, clarification of roles, responsibilities and delegations of authority, collaboration between cybersecurity experts, professions and functions, cooperation with cybersecurity experts in the conduct of industrial or commercial digital transformation projects, or in M&A operations, as well as decision-making processes are essential to the success of the company and its sustainable performance.

A cybersecurity program deployed in all departments, sites and subsidiaries is required in all large companies.

In SMEs, the organization is less complex. Nevertheless, training, safety culture, identification of strategic assets, consideration of safety rules in conjunction with IT service providers, risk mapping by managers and awareness of the importance of processes are essential. It is an investment in time rather than tools. The use of trusted service providers is essential. A list of good practices is provided in Appendix 2.

5.4. Data protection

Data governance begins with each business identifying critical assets and classifying the degree of confidentiality of information. It is not necessary to treat all information in the same way.

Sharing information is essential for greater efficiency: there is no need for each department to enter information from another department into its own database. It is a waste of time that is costly and error-prone. Two sources of information may provide different information.

It is common in large companies that information is not shared for reasons of power (information is power), frequency of updates (the requirements from one function to another are not the same), scope, confidentiality, level of quality required or organization (availability of people who update databases).

Digital transformation requires a shared vision, resources, process implementation, and change management so that it can lead to greater efficiency and reliability.

With regard to processes, it is necessary to designate persons in charge, give reading or writing rights, manage the updating of these accesses, secure access, safeguard data, ensure data integrity (document changes, for example), prevent data from being altered or destroyed, ensure their consistency, reliability, and relevance, administer and monitor logs and flows (control access, track activity, manage data violations, reduce vulnerabilities, make them anonymous if necessary, etc.).

In your opinion, does securing data stored in the cloud require specific tools or devices?

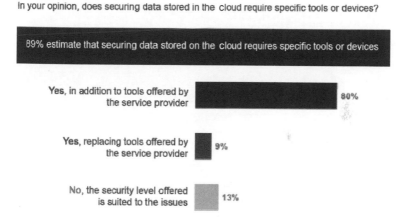

Figure 5.5. *To secure data stored in a public cloud, the CISO does not only use the tools offered by the service provider (source: according to CESIN)*

5.4.1. *Emails*

Mail has never been totally confidential, and it has always been necessary to take precautions to ensure that a letter, information or contract is known only to a few people (the sender and recipient only, the two signatories of a contract only). It is the same with email, but what is the proportion of people who are aware of it?

How to control the flow of information within a company? How to ensure that emails written today to a customer or supplier do not turn against the company in the event of a dispute? How to limit the legal and financial impacts? How to ensure compliance with the delegations of authority in place, defining the authorizations and responsibilities of each person according to the position in the company, the employment contract and the employer legal entity?

Today, who knows who wrote what about a given project? Are information flows known and managed? Are there any rules and authorizations? It is usually in the event of a dispute, audit or judicial investigation that we are aware of the amount of emails exchanged on a project.

Some have understood it well; they never write, they never answer: they are sure they will not be caught. But how do they exercise their responsibilities? Not everything is risky, however. Writing with the knowledge that emails and attachments can be read, and wondering who might misuse them, are the basic rules of their use.

Unlike some secure messaging (but beware, WhatsApp messaging was considered secure and does not seem to be), which encrypts communications, email is not secure.

We must therefore find tools – they exist – and put them in place. Some solutions are recommended for this purpose[2]:

– ProtonMail: based in Switzerland, ProtonMail is an open source webmail with a sleek design that offers different levels of encryption. Between ProtonMail users, messages are automatically encrypted end-to-end (content and attachments). It is also possible to send end-to-end encrypted messages to users of other messaging systems;

– Tutanota, based in Germany, is an open-source webmail similar to ProtonMail. The design is quite sober and elegant. Between Tutanota users, messages are automatically encrypted from start to finish. Strong authentication is available;

---

2 Source: Gilbert Kallenborn, article published on April 13, 2019, in 01Net.com.

– Mailfence, based in Belgium, is a proprietary webmail service. Its design is less pleasant than the two previous ones, but it is effective. Messages can be encrypted end-to-end using OpenPGP or symmetric encryption. Strong authentication is available.

5.4.2. *The tools*

It is not always easy with "old" systems, nor with tools commonly used, published by Microsoft (Active Directory, for example). The ANSSI technical note, dated 2014, states: "It is important to note that an Active Directory contains user secrets, such as their identification information. In fact, it is a privileged target for a malicious person".

Active Directory is Microsoft's implementation of directory services for Windows operating systems. The main objective of Active Directory is to provide centralized identification and authentication services to a network of computers using the Windows system. It also allows policy allocation and enforcement, as well as the installation of critical updates by administrators.

If he/she has domain administration rights, an attacker is free to carry out all the desired operations, such as data extraction or sabotage. The compromise of a single account with privileged rights can thus result in the loss of total control of the information system.

The complexity of this directory is such that a malicious individual can hide his/her presence in it in various more or less subtle and, for some, difficult to detect ways.

Such an individual is then able to leave backdoors in multiple services and applications of the information system. This results in a significant risk of persistent complex attacks.

An information system that has been compromised in this way is sometimes impossible to clean up and must be completely rebuilt, requiring significant financial and human resources.

Therefore, it is essential to control and secure your Active Directory. The main protection tools must be adapted to the value of the data and the criticality of the information system.

Protection tools (antivirus and firewall) are the essential basis, to be updated daily and automatically, as well as "abnormal" behavior detection tools, which analyze download behavior and suspicious actions on workstations or servers, not to mention filtering tools, which monitor inputs and outputs, to detect malicious intrusions.

There is no 100% safe system, so you have to detect those who try to pass and detect them as quickly as possible: during the day; it is much better than five years later: the consequences are not the same.

It is possible to outsource and share this monitoring. The types of tools to identify, protect, detect, react and restore are listed in Appendix 3.

5.4.3. Double authentication: better, but not 100% reliable

The use of two-factor authentication is recommended. Used by banks, it now concerns more and more sensitive companies: double authentication consists of sending a code to your smartphone, by SMS or via an application, when you try to connect to one of your online accounts or your workstation. This technique offers an additional layer of protection, in principle very reliable: who else can have your phone and reproduce the code you received?

Unfortunately, if a malicious person finds the mail from your operator sending you your SIM card or obtains a copy of your SIM card by stealing your identity, the SMS messages you receive will be displayed on your hacker's phone. While it is necessary for them to find your username and password (badly) hidden in your contacts, sometimes this is not so difficult, as most users, to simplify access to their applications, have a unique password.

5.5. Choosing your service providers

Responsibility cannot be delegated to external service providers; the company and its corporate officers remain liable in the event of an IT incident. Qualifications (products and services) have been put in place by security agencies based on criteria of competence and trust, both of which are necessary.

IT is often managed partially or totally by external parties, who have too many access rights to administer the systems of large companies.

It is the providers who are targeted to reach their customers. It is then difficult to distinguish an authorized connection from an unauthorized connection. Cyber requirements must therefore be included in providers' contracts.

5.6. The budget

It generally represents between 5% and 10% of the budget of the information systems department but varies according to the company's activity: it is higher for defense players, OIVs, companies whose intellectual property is important and which possess a lot of personal data, its level of digitization and its age.

The budget includes four main items: cyber defense (protection, detection, response), technical means maintenance, process evolution and information, awareness and training campaigns.

In large companies in particular, the rationalization of the number of providers of cybersecurity tools and services, such as the selection of interoperable tools, makes it possible to optimize investment and service budgets, to focus efforts on technology watch, surveillance tools and artificial intelligence, the resources made available to operations and functions to ensure the roles of business partner and "temple guardian" from the start of projects.

Cybersecurity should not be seen only as a cost; it should be seen as a lever for doing business, a tool for competitiveness and performance and a barometer of the organization's good health.

As with any investment, executives and administrators will be able to track expenses related to digital transformation, IT security and data protection.

An investment or innovation committee may be set up for a limited period of time, with specific skills, to set up a technology watch, supervise a start-up laboratory or accelerator, manage digital projects, costs, risks and their performance. This committee may also be responsible for compliance, internal governance, risk and insurance matters.

5.7. Cyberculture

All connected, all involved, all responsible: the cybersecurity manager is an essential business partner of the company. Cybersecurity is everyone's business. Regulators and investors are paying particular attention to how companies rely on talent and culture to improve their performance and ensure their sustainability.

The new English governance code recommends that boards of directors evaluate the culture and monitor its evolution. Similarly, the Netherlands and Japan have revised their codes of governance and insist on the importance of culture: how to define it, measure it and monitor its evolution.

COSO, which brings together various American associations of accountants and internal auditors and provides guidance on enterprise risk management, recognizes the fundamental role of corporate culture in risk management. COSO emphasizes the role of the board of directors and management in ensuring that the company's values are defined and that this culture is disseminated throughout the company, in particular by ensuring that the rules and the application of these rules are in line with this culture. Leadership by example is virtuous; "do as I say, don't do as I do" is a doorway to many negligent or malicious acts, which is very destructive of value.

What applies to culture, in general, applies to cyberculture: the composition, dynamics and culture of the board of directors itself must reflect the corporate culture and its strategic objectives. What about a board of directors that promotes digital transformation, cybersecurity and innovation if it has not acquired the appropriate skills and appointed a leader capable of leading this transformation, understanding the issues and controlling the risks? Do they spend enough time on it? Has the method of remuneration evolved in line with these new paradigms?

The dispersion of professions and the lack of employee support create a significant gap between cybersecurity practices and the cyberculture desired by companies.

For all companies, cultural adherence to cybersecurity is essential, but in practice, employees, who are usually the only barrier against phishing attacks, do not have the necessary culture to protect their company.

As revealed by the survey conducted by the Audit Guide to Digital Enterprise Information System Governance (ISACA), 95% of companies believe that there is a gap between their current cybersecurity culture and the desired culture. In practice, employees are not sufficiently trained, if at all, and can be negligent, confirming that the human aspect of cybersecurity remains essential.

Yet, 80% of organizations report that they train their employees and communicate rules of behavior to improve their cyberculture. But the reference study shows that the latter is lacking. While the cybersecurity culture is "desirable", it is limited by the lack of employee buy-in at 41% and the disparity of business units at 39%.

Cybersecurity is not only a matter for the CIO and CISO. The ISACA survey shows that cultural changes are the responsibility of CIOs, as well as of human resources. To share the sense of responsibility for security and to bridge the gap, the security culture must be inclusive, which means that it is recommended to involve employees in cybersecurity discussions, define security protocols for new employees as early as their integration process, define security needs based on departmental risk profiles and organize simulated cyber-attack exercises.

5.8. The dashboard for officers and directors

The dashboard is a good practice. It must, of course, be adapted to the type of company (its sector of activity), its size and the recipients. It must be considered as a work tool, a communication tool and a decision-making tool. It will be more or less synthetic depending on the recipients: board of directors, executive committee, business lines, IT department, CISO. It will evolve according to needs, priorities and understanding of the issues. It will be shared with each member of the executive committee. It is important to indicate who is responsible for the information provided and the actions taken.

An example of a dashboard is provided in Appendix 1.

– Have written procedures been distributed to all staff on data, systems and mobile equipment?

– Are cyber incidents reported spontaneously (safe environment)?

– Do the functions (IT, HR, legal and compliance) and business lines create a culture of cybersecurity and responsibility? Are regular training and information provided to implement instructions and recognize threats?

– What HR policies are there in terms of recruitment, training, mobility and understanding of cyber issues?

– Are access controls, encryption, back-ups, traffic monitoring, etc. in place and effective?

Box 5.2. *Best practices: the five questions to be asked regularly*

6

Resilience and Crisis Management

6.1. How to ensure resilience?

Among the organizations that manage a large CSIRP, 54% (53% in France) do not conduct regular stress tests. More than one in two organizations admit to having been the target of an incident or data breach in the past 12 months.

However, according to another IBM-sponsored Ponemon Institute study, companies that contained a data breach in less than 30 days saved more than $1 million on the total cost of the incident.

Guides or assessment tools have been developed for SMEs by national information system security agencies (or equivalent) to help companies assess their needs and put in place the main measures to ensure the company's resilience.

The Swiss Confederation has developed an ICT standard, which provides Swiss companies, particularly critical infrastructure operators in Switzerland, with guidelines for improving the resilience of their IT systems and infrastructures to cyber-risks.

The standard includes a reference guide with organizational or technical principles to protect against cyber threats. In addition, it provides a tool that allows companies to assess the degree of their IT resilience (or have it audited by external parties).

It also provides companies with a framework that provides users with a series of concrete measures to implement: identify, protect, detect (set up permanent network monitoring to detect potential cybersecurity incidents, as well as to ensure that malware can be detected), react, ensure that the lessons learned from previous cybersecurity incidents are integrated into their response plans and recover (restore back-ups, restart systems).

In your opinion, is your company prepared to manage a large-scale cyber-attack?
Basis: group (174)

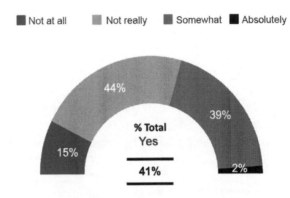

Figure 6.1. *Preparing for a major cyber-attack: less than one in two companies feels able to manage such a cyber-attack (source: according to CESIN). For a color version of this figure, see www.iste.co.uk/defreminville/cybersecurity.zip*

Finally, a database will also allow a company to compare itself anonymously with others in its sector. This standard exists for the electricity sector.

The development of a minimum IT security standard for energy suppliers is seen as a way to reduce the vulnerability of the Swiss energy sector to cyber-attack that could lead to a cyber blackout. After the electricity sector, other sectors will follow, including waste water disposal, gas supply, logistics and telecommunications.

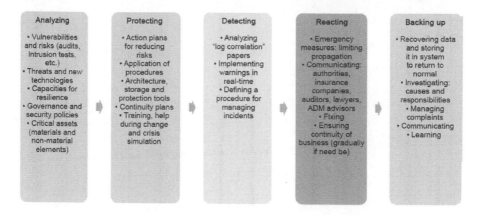

Figure 6.2. *Cyber resilience (source: Starboard Advisory)*

6.2. Definition of a CERT

The CERT (Computer Emergency Response Team) is a competence center in charge of alerts and reactions to cyber-attacks. It centralizes requests for assistance following security incidents, processes alerts, establishes and maintains a database of vulnerabilities, disseminates information on precautions to be taken to minimize risks and ensures coordination with other entities such as network competence centers, operators and Internet service providers and national and international CERTs.

CERT's mission is continuous improvement: a better understanding of the situation in order to be able to anticipate and react quickly.

6.3. Definition of a SOC

The SOC (Security Operations Center) is a supervision system whose purpose is to ensure the detection and analysis of incidents, as well as to define the response strategy to the security incident.

Its experts continuously analyze the events reported by the system and identify potential cybersecurity risks. Its main objective is to provide 24/7 monitoring of the information system. Large companies sometimes have their own SOC, but these services are often outsourced and shared, allowing experts to have a multi-company vision.

6.4. The role of ENISA

In addition, the European Parliament and the Council of Europe jointly agreed in September 2017 to provide the European Union with robust cybersecurity, based on resilience, deterrence and defense measures. This European cyber resilience strategy has given the European Network and Information Security Agency (ENISA) a permanent and broadened mandate to strengthen the European Union's cyber resilience and response capacity to cyberspace challenges, in particular through regular monitoring of the threat landscape and a response capacity to cross-border incidents.

– Strengthen "hygiene" in general: disseminate good practices within the company, train and inform, remain vigilant (new forms of attacks, new risks).

– Set up the organization, rules and methods, tools.

– Identify and protect critical data and systems. Limit access to confidential company data. Arbitrate opportunities versus risks at the highest level of the company, the data concerned being core business data.

– Conduct audits: test and estimate the level of risk (National cybersecurity agencies certifies auditors).

– Third parties: clarify the legal environment by defining internal and external responsibilities (e.g. IT service providers). Challenge the level of security promised by IT solution providers. Use products and service providers certified by National cybersecurity agencies.

Box 6.1. *The conditions of resilience: five points to remember*

6.5. The business continuity plan

Messaging, contacts, critical tools and vital information are to be identified before the crisis. The only solution is to put yourself in a situation: imagine that tomorrow morning, your email system will no longer work, you will no longer have access to your contacts, your state-of-the-art production plant will be shut down, you will no longer be able to provide services (such as banking) to your customers, your storage or delivery provider's information systems will be blocked by a ransom software, your customers' personal data (passport, social security or credit card numbers) will be stolen, while the files you are working on (legal and tax consulting firms) will be inaccessible for three weeks.

Given the potential consequences of cyber incidents or attacks, their sometimes systemic nature, and the speed with which it is necessary to be able to react, it is essential to prepare for the crisis. This preparation also has virtues: it makes it possible to become aware, build scenarios, identify risks and assess the level of this risk, then set up the action plan to be deployed on the day of the crisis and finally consider the measures to be taken to avoid a major crisis.

It is therefore necessary to identify the key functions and key people, internally and externally, to prepare for this crisis management and to be able to set up the procedures for D-Day. Who is in charge of what and when? Who should be informed – should the board of directors be informed? Depending on the severity of the crisis, who will inform the board of directors? What will be the internal communication strategy at all levels of the company and externally?

Each company will build specific crisis scenarios, which will depend on its activities, infrastructure and organization.

In the event of an attack or IT incident, the most important thing is to ensure business continuity: restarting systems and restoring data. Strict procedures and rules will have to be applied.

6.6. Crisis management

6.6.1. *The preparation*

Several questions arise regarding crisis preparedness:

– When does the crisis start and how do we identify the starting point and how do we make a quick diagnosis?

– Do employees know what to do when the alarm goes off?

– Have any exercises been done?

– How can we avoid losing track of the history so that we can be covered by insurance or take responsibility?

– Are we able to restore a recent back-up?

– Do we have the means to communicate internally? A tool, a messaging system and contacts, for example? If we do not have a digital or paper record of our contacts, we will not be able to call anyone. How many phone numbers do we know by heart? Fewer and fewer.

As with fires, or man overboard exercises in boats, the most effective way is to simulate and repeat. Even if the exercise sometimes makes you smile and the concentration is not optimal, these simulations allow you to become aware, to prepare procedures with all the teams concerned and to repeat some essential actions.

Large companies, especially vital operators, practice these exercises, which have several objectives:

– imagining scenarios, defining the first steps;

– identifying the key people in the company to manage the crisis (they will be 100% available). Their schedules and telephone numbers must be recorded. These people must have an identified back-up, relay the information, inform partners (lawyers, service providers), authorities (The National Cyber Security Centre [NCSC], ICO), according to the type of impact, the type of company (size, sector of activity) and taking decisions. Decision-making circuits must be short and organized around the CIO;

– testing the participants' ability to manage technical (network outages) and organizational problems (communicate the incident to all service providers affected by the attack) and debriefing with the teams;

– preparing emergency means of communication: secure messaging;

– communicating: what are the impacts? What incidents have occurred? What data has been leaked? The communication is aimed at employees, the press and stakeholders.

6.6.2. *Exiting the state of sideration*

We know that a cyber crisis can happen, just as a fire can happen, or a person can fall off a boat into the sea.

If the actions have been prepared in advance, and the crisis has been simulated, as seriously as possible, panic will be controlled and the action plan will proceed as planned.

The crisis will never be exactly the one that has been simulated: the place where it occurs, the first people involved, the time at which it occurs.

Being aware that this crisis can occur makes it possible to anticipate the "response": the first measures to prevent the crisis from spreading, the restoration of the activity, the balance sheet (loss of data, systems, damaged equipment, financial losses), investigations and the search for responsibilities, internal and external communication.

One of the most important levers is trust. If one is prepared for all possible scenarios, the side effect will be reduced and the ability to react will be intact.

6.6.3. *Ensuring business continuity*

The first emergency is to restore the company's ability to produce, sell, pay and be paid.

The ability to restore systems very quickly is not always possible. In this case, it is necessary to set up an ability to work in degraded (or very degraded) mode.

The testimony of Yves Bigot, one of the only business leaders who agreed to testify about the attack on TV5 Monde in April 2015, is of great value: the following testimony comes from a conference organized by HEC Gouvernance in 2017 and from various articles published in the press following this attack.

All screens have gone black. All systems and stocks could have been destroyed if the attacked machine had not been disconnected immediately. "The company could have been completely destroyed", says Yves Bigot, the channel's general manager.

The inability to restart very quickly gave TV5 Monde broadcasters the legal possibility to interrupt their broadcasting contracts. The number one objective was therefore to deliver content, regardless of the quality of the content.

ANSSI stayed with its teams for six weeks within TV5 Monde to understand the course of the attack and help restore services. It should be noted that TV5 Monde had protection deemed "correct" by ANSSI. "We are fortunate", says Yves Bigot, who acknowledges a "mental unpreparedness".

However, by its own admission, the information system is not yet 100% secure. "It's a very long and tedious job. We are still in the process of deploying our protection system and hardening it regularly, in stages. The first few months were appalling for us because the installation of these new systems produces side effects".

Financially, this security has a cost: about 4% of TV5 Monde's total budget. A legitimate cost according to Yves Bigot: "There is a real danger, but the problem is that it is immaterial. Everyone is concerned by this issue and, at the same time, not everyone is ready to take the necessary steps to protect themselves".

Following the crisis, the teams had to continue working without the Internet for almost six months, working methods were changed on a long-term basis, particularly as regards the exchange of information, documents and television productions, while physical security was also significantly improved.

6.6.4. *Story of the TV5 Monde attack*

For the first time, the agents sent to the television channel's rescue in 2015 tell how they responded to this unprecedented cyber-attack.

On April 8, 2015, around three in the morning. In the Mercure tower, the ultra-secure Parisian premises of ANSSI, a telephone rings. At the end of the line, TV5 Monde. The technicians of the French-speaking television channel have been fighting for a handful of hours against an unprecedented computer attack: the website and accounts on social networks broadcast jihadist propaganda, the image production system is unusable and the broadcasting is interrupted. The channel, which broadcasts in 200 countries for 50 million viewers, displays a black screen.

At dawn, a meeting is held. Around the table, TV5 Monde teams, the national police unit specializing in cybercrime, the domestic intelligence services and ANSSI. This agency, which is responsible for defending the State's critical IT systems and the most sensitive companies, is not theoretically involved in an attack on a television channel. But the episode was unprecedented, already public and touched one of the "voices of France" in the world: the decision was taken to send ANSSI's "computer firefighters" to the station's premises as a matter of urgency.

These interventions are common for these agents, who carry out similar operations about 20 times a year. In normal times, these maneuvers – in critical companies or fundamental state systems – are carried out in complete secrecy. TV5 Monde is a special case: the damage was immediate and highly visible. This was the first time that the work of ANSSI agents came to light so much. Two years after this incident, they presented in detail this intervention at the Symposium on Information and Communications Security (SSTIC) in Rennes on June 9. This was the first time that ANSSI has done such an exercise in public.

It was also the first time that ANSSI had publicly given itself the opportunity to share its experience.

During the first 48 hours, the agents – between 9 and 15, who were mobilized for several weeks – looked for the most obvious clues left by the attackers. Like bomb disposal experts who criss-cross the streets after the departure of an enemy army, they also feared the presence of "logic bombs", lines of code left by the attackers, designed to be activated when infected systems are restarted and intended to further paralyze the network. This fear did not materialize in the end.

From the very first hours of the investigation, agents' attention was drawn to an account name in English on TV5 Monde's computer network, configured in French and with very broad powers. Problem: it does not belong to TV5 Monde's technical teams but to pirates. The investigators managed to reconstruct its last actions and realized that it had connected to an unknown server on the Internet, outside TV5 Monde's network. They got their hands on the IP address, the identifier of this server on the Internet. A first piece of a huge puzzle to try to understand who was behind this attack.

During their investigations, ANSSI agents collected large quantities of data to analyze, including the progress of all actions carried out by hackers on the network. It took them several weeks to understand in detail how the attackers were able to penetrate TV5 Monde's networks and destroy almost everything in their path.

The course of the attack. The offensive began on January 23. The attackers observed, from a distance, TV5 Monde's network infrastructure. They discovered that it was possible to connect to the chain's internal network from outside, using a virtual private network (VPN). This is what they did, by means of the identifier and password belonging to a subcontractor in the chain. How did they obtain this information? It is one of the few unknowns in the investigation. The fact remained that the attackers had infiltrated TV5 Monde's network, which they were carefully monitoring.

Once inside, they granted themselves full powers: this tracking allowed them to locate two very specific servers, which control the cameras on the television sets. Hackers used one of these two servers to connect to the system, which was responsible for determining what each computer on the network is allowed to do or not to do. The grail: once inside, it was possible for them to grant themselves full powers.

Then, the pirates snooped around. They immersed themselves in the internal documentation of TV5 Monde's IT departments and their messaging and search for any information that would allow them to continue their infiltration. The keywords they entered were precise: they wanted to know how the network was organized and configured, and more specifically, the one that manages the video streams broadcast by the channel. From the beginning, they were interested in the French-language channel's image distribution system.

This harvest was successful, and hackers recovered a lot of information, including IDs and passwords from various machines. For several weeks, the pirates were very discreet. No activity was recorded in this interval. ANSSI officials suspected that this period was spent analyzing, understanding and even translating the data collected. It was only to come back better, first to check the validity of the recovered elements. The attackers checked that the passwords for accessing social networks worked well. It was then April 6, two days before the attack itself.

On April 8, at 3:40 p.m., the hackers made a final check on TV5 Monde's network. They placed standard spyware software in a prominent place. Strangely, the latter was never activated. According to ANSSI officials, it was possible that this malware, widely accessible to anyone online, was left to be used as a decoy and to mislead investigators.

The beginning of the offensive. At 7:57 p.m., the assailant started his demolition business. He modified the parameters of the multiplexers – the computers that manage and direct the chain's heavy video streams – to make it impossible to restart them. This change was invisible until the latter were switched off, and the channel continued to transmit. The first visible action occurred at 8:58 p.m., when accounts on social networks took on the colors of a mysterious "cyber caliphate" and showed their support for the "Islamic State" organization. All TV5 Monde video streams were interrupted, and the screens turned black.

At 9:48 p.m., another assault. The attackers connected to several critical parts of TV5 Monde's network and destroyed the software that made them operate. All TV5 Monde video streams were interrupted, and the screens turned black.

In its misfortune, TV5 Monde was lucky: a new thematic channel had just been launched, and many technicians were still on the premises at a late hour to celebrate its arrival. They reacted immediately. Their task was complicated by a new attack by hackers, who suppressed the company's internal messaging at 10:40 p.m. At this point, TV5 Monde's teams had completely lost control of their network. Shortly before midnight, they took the only possible decision to stop the attack: they completely isolated it from the rest of the world.

The pirates lost their hand, but it was in a field of digital ruins that ANSSI agents arrived in the early morning. They came to help the helpless but competent and very cooperative technical teams. Never had ANSSI experts, whose discretion was proverbial, had to face such media pressure. Television cameras camped in front of the entrance of the television channel. TV5 Monde journalists, whose workplace made the headlines, tried to extract information from them, to the detriment of the extreme sensitivity of these first hours of investigation. Officers needed to seal the glass doors of their crisis room, set up for the occasion, so as not to be seen, flee the cameras in the corridors, and even take refuge under their desk to hide their screens when the cameras broke into the room.

ANSSI agents and TV5 Monde teams were working to regain control of their network. Their task was also technically complex. To understand the attackers' modus operandi, they needed to familiarize themselves very quickly with equipment specific to the audiovisual sector. While the attackers have had several weeks, the deadlines imposed on ANSSI agents could be counted in hours. The objective was set as soon as they arrived: we must resume broadcasting as soon as possible and offer employees a temporary but secure solution to work. And above all, do everything possible to ensure that hackers do not set foot in the channel's network again. The pressure was enormous: every minute that passed without satellite broadcasting cost the television channel thousands of euros.

The first healthy computers were installed for TV5 Monde journalists. From that evening, at 8:00 p.m., TV5 Monde broadcasted again, but only with pre-recorded content. In the meantime, the clean-up began: infected machines were discarded and replaced by new equipment. The agents set up a small room so that journalists could resume their work: five Macs with an explicit sticker: "Absolute and unconditional prohibition: do not connect anything".

At this stage, ANSSI agents were still afraid that the pirates would return. As the days went by, workstations were added and soon formed the new newsroom for journalists. For weeks, the chain's employees were traumatized by this episode: a wave of panic blew over the company when the ANSSI canceled passwords that were too old and therefore vulnerable. They then became unusable, and many journalists believed that the pirates were back.

A high-risk scale. For one month, ANSSI agents, TV5 Monde teams and their subcontractors worked to map the network and prepare the switchover to a secure system, free of traces of the attack. The latter took place on May 11, one month after the attack. From 5 p.m. to 5 a.m., they carried out this extremely delicate operation without being able to disconnect the network, because TV5 Monde could not – once again – stop broadcasting. The experts even had to interrupt their technical operations every four hours to avoid disrupting the broadcasting of news programs.

The two years after this turbulent episode have been instructive. The hackers took advantage of security breaches: TV5 Monde had outsourced large parts of its network to subcontractors, diluting knowledge about the network, and some basic good practices were not being followed. But these defects are identical in most large French companies, the ANSSI agents say, who are well placed to know this.

The attack on TV5 Monde also fueled the concerns of these state experts. "There is a real awareness of the importance of information technology in our modern societies", explains one of ANSSI's agents on stage at SSTIC: "There were several warning shots, TV5 Monde was one of them. Today, no attacker really wanted to kill anyone in France, but keep in mind that one day it could hurt a lot".

In total, this attack will have cost the television channel approximately €20 million over five years. Who is behind this attack? As usual, ANSSI did not make any suggestions on this eminently political issue, leaving it to the judicial inquiry, opened by the anti-terrorist prosecutor's office on the evening of the attack, to trace it back to possible leaders or sponsors.

The latter, despite the claims posted on the channel's website and social networks, turned to the pirate group APT28 that had learned of *Le Monde* from a judicial source in June 2015. The latter is suspected of being the armed arm of the Kremlin on the Internet.

6.6.5. *Management of the first few hours*

6.6.5.1. *Emergency measures*

The first few hours should be devoted to emergency measures: alerting IT and IT security experts before abruptly disconnecting the devices on which the incidents have been observed, communicating internally and externally, notifying the authorities (ANSSI, ICO if necessary), preserving evidence, for reasons of responsibility and insurance.

The CIO and CISO will make decisions to block the spread and isolate what has been affected, the company's critical systems and sites and, if necessary, stop them to ensure this separation.

Indeed, it is better to stop the activity for one day to protect the most critical sites and activities and restart what can be restored.

Regular communication to the company's managers and executives should be ensured by a person designated in advance, with explanations of incidents and impacts, information on restoration measures and a provisional schedule. The practical aspects of the teams involved in system protection and restoration must also be organized.

The list of persons to contact must be established before the crisis: do not forget the legal department and lawyers, the general management, the board of directors (has the board of directors indicated the degree of seriousness at which it wishes to be informed?), an independent judicial investigator, the insurance company, the external auditors, the crisis communication advisor, who will have been identified before a crisis occurs (the cost of his/her intervention will be lower; he/she will know the company, its activity and the main risks), without forgetting investors and clients.

Silence generally reigns after cyber-attacks: a laconic press release and then great silence.

The case of Hydro, which was hit in March 2019 by the same malware as Altran, is different from this point of view: Hydro communicated widely as soon as the attack occurred and informed the public of the measures taken. Once its site was reopened, Hydro regularly informed its customers, suppliers and investors of the costs (the website indicates a financial impact of between 40 and 50 million euros for the first quarter of 2019), progress and outstanding issues. In particular, Hydro asks them to be extremely vigilant when they receive requests from the company, for example, to modify bank accounts and to contact Hydro services to verify the origin of this request.

As Frédéric Charles (Green SI) tells us:

> From March 19 until early April, the company published a dedicated page on its website with a press release and regular updates. A press web conference was also held on March 19 to give a situation of the impact on the company's various activities and inform that energy production was not affected.

Transparency was also provided on the return to manual procedures to continue processing the right production orders. The business continuity plan obviously worked.

On April 2, when everything was much better, the company even launched a video on YouTube where the employees of the first affected site told how they experienced it. They explained how they understood that something serious was going on, how they all contributed to the continuity of the service regardless of their profession and how they spent nights and a weekend restarting their business.

This attack will have cost at least $40 million in lost revenue and additional IT service costs to restart the IS for two weeks, but other costs will certainly appear for several months to come. Hydro announced that it had not paid the ransom, which would have been an additional cost.

An insurance policy taken out with AIG will cover part of this operating loss. The stock price has returned to the same level after falling at the beginning of the crisis.

This crisis that Hydro has had to face is instructive both for the way the communication was organized and for:

– IT architecture: avoid the lack of centralized IT. Indeed, the Active Directory, necessarily centralized, was the means for the rapid spread of the virus;

– connections between the company's information system and those of production systems: to be avoided to prevent the spread of infection. It is therefore necessary to organize the flow of information between the company's departments and the production sites (in both directions) so that the sites are not affected;

– the measures taken: isolate the malware to prevent it from spreading further;

– measures to restore back-ups workstation by workstation because the ransomware had modified administrator access on each infected workstation.

The Norsk Hydro Group's Norwegian board of directors postponed the publication of its first quarter results to June 5 (instead of April 30) due to the cyber-attack, which caused delays in some administrative processes, including reporting and billing systems.

6.6.5.2. *The payment of the ransom*

On May 8, 2019, the "Robin Hood" ransom software blocked many computer systems in the city of Baltimore, United States. The hackers behind the attack demanded a ransom in exchange for the decryption, which was refused by the city authorities, who do not want to give in to blackmail. Two weeks later, the administrative services are still blocked: payment of taxes, access to emails, surrender of permits or allocation of property. The hackers have taken control of 10,000 computers belonging to the city.

According to experts, the recovery of services could take from several weeks to several months for the most complex systems: "our objective is to restore the most important services, while ensuring maximum security so that the attack cannot happen again", says the mayor of Baltimore.

It is not advisable, as explained above, to pay the ransoms. However, in addition to antivirus software, updates and limited access to unsecured sites or applications, it is recommended to train employees and organize daily automatic back-ups in two different locations, test the quality of the back-ups and protect recovery programs to prevent them from being infected by a virus.

6.6.5.3. *Medium-term management*

Once the emergency measures have been taken, the time has come for investigations: investigation of causes and responsibilities, declarations to insurance companies, recurrent internal and external communications on the facts and improvement of security processes and devices to prevent a recurrence of the incident.

6.6.5.4. *Long-term management*

Corrective actions, litigation management, feedback and improvement of security and data protection, as well as communication management will be on the company's agenda and should not be neglected:

– What are the main lessons: how did we discover the incident? From the outside? Or internally?

– Do we have any information on what was stolen? Deteriorated?

– What were the impacts?

– Have any operations been compromised?

– Did our crisis management plan work as planned?

– Who was notified? Who should be notified? Is the legal department involved and prepared?

– What actions have been taken to ensure that attackers no longer have access to data? Do we have any idea who the hacker is?

– What vulnerabilities have been exploited by the attacker? And why is that?

– What actions can be taken to avoid a second attack of the same type?

– What actions can be taken to reduce the impact of this incident?

6.7. Crisis simulation

The best crisis preparation is through crisis simulation. It makes it possible to become aware of the impacts of an attack, to prepare response plans, emergency measures and the formation of teams.

As with fire or earthquake exercises, some sensitive companies have simulated cyber crises, which test the procedures prepared to deal with a crisis.

Crisis scenarios must be adapted to the business sector, process and location of the company, and therefore be inspired by cyber-risk mapping, to be as likely and effective as possible (ransom request and inability to access data, inaccessible website, unavailable messaging, production site down, cloud provider out of service).

Crisis scenarios make it possible to experiment with the overall management of a crisis or to check the maturity of the teams in order to react without panicking, collectively, and according to procedures prepared in advance:

– emergency management (avoidance of spread);

– activation of crisis systems and teams;

– application of procedures;

– crisis communication (media, clients, staff, authorities, etc.);

– continuity and business recovery.

The simulation of all teams, infrastructures and tools allows us to test and improve the processes and reflexes, as well as the programs to be implemented in case of an incident. The incidents will never be the same, but the reactions will be similar.

– Set up a crisis team (IT, legal, HR, communication, insurance) with the means to reach them at all times.

– Plan detailed b plans for each activity, configure an emergency messaging system that can be used by management and plan logistics for the IT team, which will be mobilized 24 hours a day for several days.

– Organize alternative production units (abroad?) and ensure that suppliers can work in a degraded mode.

– Negotiate with your service provider to provide PCs on an emergency basis.

– Plan for the auditors, lawyers, communicators to be mobilized and the procedures to be covered by insurance.

Box 6.2. *Crisis management: five recommendations*

Conclusion

The Digital Committee

So long as the Internet is not regulated and governed, users (individuals and businesses) will remain insecure. Governments must balance the protection of human rights with the monitoring of communications in the name of security (terrorism, pedophilia, etc.).

In addition, new technologies are used in international conflicts (commercial or political) to spy and sabotage. End-to-end encryption techniques make it difficult to intercept communications, and therefore to infiltrate intelligence networks.

There is therefore no such thing as zero risk. Nevertheless, it is essential for boards and executives to be involved in this strategic subject: digital transformation creates value if security issues are addressed upstream, and informed decisions are made, which requires that executives and directors have the skills to understand and guide strategy in an informed way.

A digital committee, based on the financial audit committee, would be a good practice. It would make it possible to audit cybersecurity systems: organizations, processes, tools, and training related to the digital strategy, just as the audit committee makes it possible, through its independence of view, to support management, in order to make the company a more competitive and efficient organization, by ensuring the quality of financial information, risk mapping and internal control. This governance body would strengthen governance practices, and thus the digital trust of stakeholders.

The digital committee would contribute, with the assistance of an independent expert (cyber auditor), to ensuring:

– the relevance of the cybersecurity system;

– the reliability of risk management and process implementation processes: identify, protect, detect, respond, restore;

– the monitoring of threats, technological developments and best practices in cybersecurity.

This digital committee would be linked to the CISO and the risk committee or audit committee to ensure that risk mapping takes into account cyber threats and vulnerabilities, as well as physical security issues.

It is likely that companies will be forced to have their cybersecurity arrangements audited in the near future, as well as the appointment of auditors is mandatory, above a certain size, which will allow the board of directors to be informed promptly of any difficulties encountered.

The digital committee may intervene or involve the cyber listener in particular operations:

– review of merger/acquisition/disposal transactions;

– security policy review;

– choice of critical suppliers;

– compliance reviews;

– post-crisis investigations.

Finally, the digital committee will be able to monitor the social and environmental impacts of the digital transformation, the development of skills and a cybersecurity culture, in line with the strategy and CSR.

Digital transformation has not yet led to a real transformation of the board of directors, either in its composition, its mode of operation or in the consideration of these new risks to be assumed.

It is time to transform the board of directors and the executive committee.

Appendices

Appendix 1

Cybersecurity Dashboard

Threats Risks Vulnerabilities
Threat status and topicality (managers). – Topical issues (cited sources). – Number of security incidents: type of attacks and impacts (non-corporate). – Number of security alerts in the company: types of attacks and impacts. – Evolution seen by the tools: scanning of data leaks on darknet and deepnet. – Type of incidents to be detailed: intrusion attempts, denial of service attacks, human errors, others. – Responsible manager.
Mapping of risks on the most exposed activities (managers). Most exposed activities to be defined with the business. By exposed activity. – Level of protection. – Monitoring tools. – Incidents observed (evolution). – Risks during treatment. – Risks not covered. – New risks discovered. – Responsible manager.
Essential points of vulnerability of the company (managers). – Number of critical vulnerabilities addressed in the previous quarter. – Number of critical vulnerabilities to be addressed as a priority. – The nature and number of vulnerabilities being fixed.

Detection-Protection-Reaction System Security Policies Projects and Security

Detection protection reaction system (responsible manager).
– Detection device: tools/teams/alert processes.
– Protection device:
  - office automation: antivirus, updates and encryption (percentage of the processed fleet);
  - application servers: antivirus, updates, encryption (percentage processed);
  - network;
  - data back-up (where, when, encryption).
– Authorization management, authentication systems.
– Physical access security.
– Reaction device.
– Crisis management system.

Security policies (responsible manager). – List and dates of documents. – Planned updates (depending on system and incident evolution function). – Audits carried out. – By audit: number of outstanding recommendations.
Company projects (managers). – Teleworking. – Website. – Cloud. – External growth operation. – Critical subcontractors.
Action Plans Resources Resources Conformity
Ongoing and future action plans (leaders). – Dates and purpose of business continuity tests. – Test results. – Intrusion tests. – Training (and staff testing): number of people trained/sensitized. – Information to staff (incidents, vigilance points, etc.).

Cybersecurity resources (responsible manager).
– Budget.
– Investments.
– Staffing.

Compliance (responsible manager).
– Complaints/litigations/alerts.
– IT service provider contracts.
– Critical suppliers.
– Regulations (NIS–GDPR–sectoral regulations).
– Ongoing actions.
– Actions to be launched.

Appendix 2

Ensuring Cybersecurity in Practice and on a Daily Basis

– Managing passwords.

– Managing access rights to systems and applications.

– Partitioning uses.

– Defining rules for digital partners and service providers.

– Regularly updating the software of all hardware.

– Training staff (including avoiding the use of a USB stick of unknown origin, installing software without prior authorization, default configurations and unused features).

– Disseminating a charter of good conduct.

– Disabling or removing default accounts, ports (USB or other) and unused removable media, non-essential web services, etc.

– Backing up data and software regularly on separate media.

– Updating operating systems and security applications.

– Controlling access to production equipment via personalized passwords.

– Protecting physical and digital access to SCADA (Supervisory Control and Data Acquisition) development stations, programming consoles, PLCs (programmable logic controllers), handheld terminals, etc.

– Mapping information flows, filtering them with firewalls, tracing and analyzing connection failures.

– Separating networks (office automation, workshops, etc.) and connections between production islands.

– Disabling remote access, vulnerable and unsecured protocols and features.

– Separating development tools from production servers or operator stations.

– Identifying the documents to be archived and the archiving conditions.

– Encrypting sensitive data.

– Testing back-up recovery processes.

– Disconnecting back-ups from the information system and keeping back-ups on multiple physical media.

– Ensuring that subcontractors meet acceptable cybersecurity requirements in relation to those required.

– Ensuring the protection of customer data, in the case of marketing connected objects, integrating appropriate encryption mechanisms.

– Having the conformity of products and services certified and audited by a third party such as a national center for IT Security Evaluation and Certification.

– Using products certified by the National Cybersecurity Agency: data erasure, secure storage, operating and virtualization systems, firewalls, intrusion detection, antivirus, malware protection, security administration and supervision, identification, authentication and access control, secure communication, secure messaging, embedded hardware and software, secure execution environment, PLCs, industrial switch.

Appendix 3

Tools to Identify, Protect, Detect, Train, React and Restore

A3.1 Identify

- Threat identification.
- Asset management.
- Vulnerability management.
- Penetration testing.

A3.2. Protecting

- Antivirus email, firewall protecting the web application server.
- IPS/IDS intrusion detection/prevention systems (IDS) analyzing network traffic to detect signatures corresponding to known cyber-attacks.
- Data: encryption/decryption tools, key management, PKI (public key infrastructure).
- Multifactor authentication.
- Identity and access management.
- Update management.

– Limiting access of certain websites to specific users in order to maintain and comply with the organization's policies and standards (endpoint protection).

– Secure DNS.

– Web filtering: limiting access to websites (threatening the organization's IT security), reducing malware infections, reducing incident tickets and reducing the burden on IT resources.

– Virtual private network (VPN) is a system that allows you to create a direct link between remote computers by isolating this traffic. This term is particularly used in teleworking, for access to cloud computing structures, as well as in MPLS (Multiprotocol Label Switching) services.

A3.3. Training and governance

– Change management.

– Governance risk and compliance monitoring.

– GDPR compliance.

– Cybersecurity training.

A3.4. Detecting

– Log management: log collection, centralized log aggregation, long-term storage and retention time, log file rotation, log analysis (in real time and in bulk after a storage period), log reports and study, network monitoring.

– Honeypot: active defense which consists of attracting, on resources (server, program, service), declared or potential opponents in order to identify them and possibly neutralize them.

– DLP (Data Loss Prevention).

– Centralized management server, which processes three types of information: moving information (broadcast by email, instant messaging, or on the Web), stored information (static data on a server) and processed information (transmitted from computers to USB sticks or by printing, for example). An internal company policy will be defined on the centralized management of this information.

– Control of email flows and redirection of sensitive emails to a manager who will then agree whether or not to send the email.

– Network controller: server that scans web activity, locates and controls information. It is able to block certain violations based on the company's internal policy and stop any undesirable activity.

– Host IDS (Intrusion Detection System) or machine intrusion detection system.

– File integrity monitoring: tracking changes to file and folder creation, access, viewing, deletion, modification, renamed files, real-time alerts on changes occurring on files and folders.

– Reverse proxy/load balancer: additional security layer for servers authenticating users through internal authentication sources.

A3.5. Reacting

Security automation and orchestration tools designed to improve the productivity and efficiency of security operation centers and analysts (collection and correlation of data from different security systems, coordination of incident response and management life cycles, incident detection and processing).

A3.6. Restoring

– Back-ups.

– Restoration.

Glossary

ANSSI: *Agence nationale de sécurité des systèmes d'information française* [French security agency for information systems]

APT: Advanced Persistent Threats, discreet and time-consuming intrusion to take data without attracting attention

BATX: Baidu, Alibaba, Tencent and Xiaomi, to which should be added the "H" of "Huawei", the Internet giants of China

Botnet: network of computer robots that perform tasks on a network

CERT: Computer Emergency Response Team

CIO: Chief Information Officer

CISO: Chief Information Security Officer

CNIL: *Commission nationale française de l'informatique et des libertés* [French regulatory body to ensure that data privacy laws are applied for the collection, storage and use of personal data]

COSO: internal control framework defined by the Committee of Sponsoring Organizations of the Treadway Commission

CRM: Customer Relationship Management

DoS: Denial-of-Service attack

ENISA: European Union Agency for Cybersecurity

ERP: Enterprise Resource Planning

FINMA: Swiss Financial Market Supervisory Authority

GAFAM: Google, Apple, Facebook, Amazon and Microsoft

GDPR: General Data Protection Regulation

IoT: Internet of Things, interconnection between the Internet and objects, places and physical environments

IT: Information Technology

LPM: French Military Programming Act

MELANI: Swiss registration and analysis center for information assurance

NIS: Network and Information Security, European directive adopted on July 6, 2016, on network and information systems security

Phishing: the fraudulent practice of sending emails apparently from reputable companies in order to induce individuals to reveal personal information, such as passwords and credit card numbers or login information

Ransomware: malicious program that locks a computer or encrypts its data in order to extort money from the user; reproduces on several computers using the network

Rootkits: they allow remote access and recording (camera)

SEC: Securities and Exchange Commission, in the United States

SIEM: Security Information and Event Management

SOC: Security Operation Center

Spyware: or malware that installs itself in a computer or mobile device to collect and transfer information about the environment in which it has settled, very often without the user's knowledge; logs keyboard and screen data

Trojan horse: a program that takes control of your computer

Virus: a program that associates itself with another program and causes it to malfunction

References

Accenture (2019). Anticiper et minimiser l'impact d'un cyber risque sur votre entreprise. Rapport 2018 de la cyber-résilience.

ANSSI (2017). Guide d'hygiène informatique [Online]. Available at: https://www.ssi.gouv.fr/guide/guide-dhygiene-informatique/.

ANSSI (2018). EBIOS Risk Manager [Online]. Available at: https://www.ssi.gouv.fr/guide/la-methode-ebios-risk-manager-le-guide/.

APIA (2018). Gouvernance et rupture numérique. *Cahier APIA*, 26.

Bessé, P. and Trouchaud, P. (2018). Les dirigeants d'ETI face à la menace cyber [Online]. Available at: https://www.pwc.fr/fr/assets/files/pdf/2018/03/etude-cyber-eti-besse-pwc.pdf.

Bonime-Blanc, A. (2016). A Strategic Cyber-Roadmap for the Board. Harvard Law School Forum on Corporate Governance and Financial Regulation.

Canard, J. (2019). Les as de la cyberdéfense ont laissé traîné leurs petits secrets sur le Web. *Le Canard enchaîné*, 13 February.

Canton de Vaud (2018). Stratégie numérique du canton de Vaud. Communiqué du Conseil d'État, Lausanne.

CEIDIG (2017). *L'essentiel de la sécurité numérique pour les dirigeants*. Eyrolles, Paris.

Centre for Cybersecurity Belgium (2014). Cybersécurité : Guide pour les PME [Online]. Available at: https://ccb.belgium.be/fr/document/guide-pour-les-pme.

CIGREF (2014). L'entreprise 2020 à l'ère du numérique. Report [Online]. Available at: https://www.cigref.fr/publications-numeriques/ebook-cigref-entreprise-2020-enjeux-efis/files/assets/common/downloads/Entreprise%202020.pdf.

CIGREF (2018). Cybersécurité : Visualiser, comprendre, décider. Report [Online]. Available at: https://www.cigref.fr/publication-cybersecurite-visualiser-comprendre-decider.

CIGREF, AFAI-ISACA, IFACI (2019). Guide d'audit de la gouvernance du système d'information de l'entreprise numérique [Online]. Available at: https://www.cigref.fr/wp/wp-content/uploads/2019/03/2019-Guide-Audit-Gouvernance-Systeme-Information-Entreprise-Numerique-2eme-edition-Cigref-Afai-Ifaci.pdf.

Collins, A. (2019). The Global Risks Report 2019. World Economic Forum Report [Online]. Available at: http://www3.weforum.org/docs/WEF_Global_Risks_Report_2019.pdf.

Collomb, G. (2018). État de la menace liée au numérique en 2018. Communiqué de presse du ministère de l'Intérieur, Paris.

Cotelle, P., Wolf, P., Suzan, B. (2017). La maîtrise du risque cyber sur l'ensemble de la chaîne de sa valeur et son transfert vers l'assurance. Résultats du séminaire de recherche novembre 2015 July 2016 [Online]. Available at: https://www.irt-systemx.fr/wp-content/uploads/2016/11/ISX-IC-EIC-transfert-ris que-LIV-0401-v10_2016-10-25.pdf.

CTI (2017). La cybersécurité et les PME manufacturières. Rapport de l'Alliance industrie du futur [Online]. Available at: http://www.industrie-dufutur.org/Documents%20%C3%A0%20t%C3%A9l%C3%A9charger/cybersecurite-pme-manufacturieres/.

CVCI (2018). Les entreprises vaudoises face aux enjeux de la cybersécurité. Study [Online]. Available at: https://www.cvci.ch/fileadmin/documents/cvci.ch/pdf/Medias/publications/divers/12315_ENQUETE_CYBERSECURITE_PROD_PP.pdf.

DCPJ (2015). Réagir à une attaque informatique, 10 préconisations. Report [Online]. Available at: https://www.cybermalveillance.gouv.fr/wp-conte nt/uploads/2017/05/Livret-B5-SDLC.pdf.

DCRO (2018). Guiding principles for cyber risks governance. Report [Online]. Available at: https://www.assured.enterprises/wpcontent/uploads/2018/06/DCRO_Cybersecurity_web.pdf.

DEFR (2018). Norme minimale pour améliorer la résilience informatique [Online]. Available at: https://www.assured.enterprises/wpcontent/uploads/2018/06/DC RO_ Cybersecurity_web.pdf.

Deloitte (2018). Assessing cyber risks. Critical questions for the board and the C-suite. Report [Online]. Available at: https://www2.deloitte.com/global/en/ pages/risk/articles/assessing-cyber-risk.html.

ENISA (2018). Cybersecurity Culture Guidelines: Behavioural Aspects of Cyber-security. Report [Online]. Available at: https://www.enisa.europa.eu/publications/ cybersecurity-culture-guidelines-behavioural-aspects-of-cybersecurity.

FERMA (2017). FERMA ECIIA Cyber Risk Governance report 29 June 2017. Report [Online]. Available at: https://www.ferma.eu/publication/ferma-eciia-cyber-risk-governance-report/.

Gergorin, J.-L. and Isaac-Dognin, L. (2018). *Cyber. La guerre permanente*. Éditions du Cerf, Paris.

Goldstein, G.-P. (2018). Cyber-risques : Enjeux, approches et gouvernance. Rapport de l'Institut français de l'audit et du contrôle interne [Online]. Available at: https://www.ifaci.com/wp-content/uploads/Cyber-risques.pdf.

IFA, KPMG (2016). Rôle du comité d'audit en matière de cybersécurité. Report [Online]. Available at: https://home.kpmg/content/dam/kpmg/pdf/2016/07/FR-ACI-IFA-Guide-Cybersecurite.pdf.

Institut Montaigne (2018). Cybermenace, avis de tempête. Report [Online]. Available at: https://www.institutmontaigne.org/publications/cybermenace-avis-de-tempete.

Jacob, M. (2019). Kit de sensibilisation aux risques numériques [Online]. Available at: https://www.cybermalveillance.gouv.fr/contenus-de-sensibilisation/.

MELANI (2018). Sécurité de l'information : Aide-mémoire pour les PME. Report [Online]. Available at: file:///C:/Users/ISTE%20asus/Downloads/180525_ MerkBlatt-Info-Sicherheit-KMU-fr.pdf.

Morgan, S. (2019). Top 5 Cybersecurity Facts, Figures, Predictions, and Statistics for 2019 to 2021. *Cybersecurityventures.com* [Online]. Available at: https://cybersecurityventures.com/top-5-cybersecurity-facts-figures-predictions-and-statistics-for-2019-to-2021/.

NACD (2017). Cyber risks oversight. Centre de ressources [Online]. Available at: https://www.nacdonline.org/insights/resource_center.cfm?ItemNumber =20789.

Palo Alto Networks (2015). Buyers guide cyber security. Guide.

Patin, D. (2017). Adopter le Cloud en toute sécurité. Guide pratique CEIS, en partenariat avec Business Digital Security et ATIPIC Avocat.

Saint-Gobain (2017). Document de référence 2017. Report [Online]. Available at: https://www.saint-gobain.com/sites/sgcom.master/files/saint-gobain-do cument-de-reference-2017.pdf.

Scor (2017). Cyber risk on the rise: From intangible threat to tangible (re)insurance solutions. Report, Scor Global P&C Strategy & Development.

Swiss Re Institute (2017). Cyber : Comment venir à bout d'un risque complexe ? Report.

Swisscom (2018). Cybersecurity 2018 : Intelligence artificielle, logiciels malveillants et crypto-monnaies. Report.

Untersinger, M. (2017). Le piratage de TV5 Monde vu de l'intérieur. *Le Monde*, 10 June [Online]. Available at: https://www.lemonde.fr/pixels/article/2017/06/10/le-piratage-de-tv5-monde-vu-de-l-interieur_5142046_4408996.html.

Index

Other titles from

in

Information Systems, Web and Pervasive Computing

2020

GEORGE Éric
Digitalization of Society and Socio-political Issues 2: Digital, Information and Research

SEDKAOUI Soraya, KHELFAOUI Mounia
Sharing Economy and Big Data Analytics

2019

ALBAN Daniel, EYNAUD Philippe, MALAURENT Julien, RICHET Jean-Loup, VITARI Claudio
Information Systems Management: Governance, Urbanization and Alignment

AUGEY Dominique, with the collaboration of ALCARAZ Marina
Digital Information Ecosystems: Smart Press

BATTON-HUBERT Mireille, DESJARDIN Eric, PINET François
Geographic Data Imperfection 1: From Theory to Applications

BRIQUET-DUHAZÉ Sophie, TURCOTTE Catherine
From Reading-Writing Research to Practice

BROCHARD Luigi, KAMATH Vinod, CORBALAN Julita, HOLLAND Scott, MITTELBACH Walter, OTT Michael
Energy-Efficient Computing and Data Centers

CHAMOUX Jean-Pierre
The Digital Era 2: Political Economy Revisited

COCHARD Gérard-Michel
Introduction to Stochastic Processes and Simulation

DUONG Véronique
SEO Management: Methods and Techniques to Achieve Success

GAUCHEREL Cédric, GOUYON Pierre-Henri, DESSALLES Jean-Louis
Information, The Hidden Side of Life

GEORGE Éric
Digitalization of Society and Socio-political Issues 1: Digital, Communication and Culture

GHLALA Riadh
Analytic SQL in SQL Server 2014/2016

JANIER Mathilde, SAINT-DIZIER Patrick
Argument Mining: Linguistic Foundations

SOURIS Marc
Epidemiology and Geography: Principles, Methods and Tools of Spatial Analysis

TOUNSI Wiem
Cyber-Vigilance and Digital Trust: Cyber Security in the Era of Cloud Computing and IoT

2018

ARDUIN Pierre-Emmanuel
Insider Threats
(Advances in Information Systems Set – Volume 10)

CARMÈS Maryse
Digital Organizations Manufacturing: Scripts, Performativity and Semiopolitics
(Intellectual Technologies Set – Volume 5)

CARRÉ Dominique, VIDAL Geneviève
Hyperconnectivity: Economical, Social and Environmental Challenges
(Computing and Connected Society Set – Volume 3)

CHAMOUX Jean-Pierre
The Digital Era 1: Big Data Stakes

DOUAY Nicolas
Urban Planning in the Digital Age
(Intellectual Technologies Set – Volume 6)

FABRE Renaud, BENSOUSSAN Alain
The Digital Factory for Knowledge: Production and Validation of Scientific Results

GAUDIN Thierry, LACROIX Dominique, MAUREL Marie-Christine, POMEROL Jean-Charles
Life Sciences, Information Sciences

GAYARD Laurent
Darknet: Geopolitics and Uses
(Computing and Connected Society Set – Volume 2)

IAFRATE Fernando
Artificial Intelligence and Big Data: The Birth of a New Intelligence
(Advances in Information Systems Set – Volume 8)

LE DEUFF Olivier
Digital Humanities: History and Development
(Intellectual Technologies Set – Volume 4)

MANDRAN Nadine
Traceable Human Experiment Design Research: Theoretical Model and Practical Guide
(Advances in Information Systems Set – Volume 9)

PIVERT Olivier
NoSQL Data Models: Trends and Challenges

ROCHET Claude
Smart Cities: Reality or Fiction

SAUVAGNARGUES Sophie
Decision-making in Crisis Situations: Research and Innovation for Optimal Training

SEDKAOUI Soraya
Data Analytics and Big Data

SZONIECKY Samuel
Ecosystems Knowledge: Modeling and Analysis Method for Information and Communication
(Digital Tools and Uses Set – Volume 6)

2017

BOUHAÏ Nasreddine, SALEH Imad
Internet of Things: Evolutions and Innovations
(Digital Tools and Uses Set – Volume 4)

DUONG Véronique
Baidu SEO: Challenges and Intricacies of Marketing in China

LESAS Anne-Marie, MIRANDA Serge
The Art and Science of NFC Programming
(Intellectual Technologies Set – Volume 3)

LIEM André
Prospective Ergonomics
(Human-Machine Interaction Set – Volume 4)

MARSAULT Xavier
Eco-generative Design for Early Stages of Architecture
(Architecture and Computer Science Set – Volume 1)

REYES-GARCIA Everardo
The Image-Interface: Graphical Supports for Visual Information
(Digital Tools and Uses Set – Volume 3)

REYES-GARCIA Everardo, BOUHAÏ Nasreddine
Designing Interactive Hypermedia Systems
(Digital Tools and Uses Set – Volume 2)

SAÏD Karim, BAHRI KORBI Fadia
Asymmetric Alliances and Information Systems:Issues and Prospects
(Advances in Information Systems Set – Volume 7)

SZONIECKY Samuel, BOUHAÏ Nasreddine
Collective Intelligence and Digital Archives: Towards Knowledge
Ecosystems
(Digital Tools and Uses Set – Volume 1)

2016

BEN CHOUIKHA Mona
Organizational Design for Knowledge Management

BERTOLO David
Interactions on Digital Tablets in the Context of 3D Geometry Learning
(Human-Machine Interaction Set – Volume 2)

BOUVARD Patricia, SUZANNE Hervé
Collective Intelligence Development in Business

EL FALLAH SEGHROUCHNI Amal, ISHIKAWA Fuyuki, HÉRAULT Laurent,
TOKUDA Hideyuki
Enablers for Smart Cities

FABRE Renaud, in collaboration with MESSERSCHMIDT-MARIET Quentin,
HOLVOET Margot
New Challenges for Knowledge

GAUDIELLO Ilaria, ZIBETTI Elisabetta
Learning Robotics, with Robotics, by Robotics
(Human-Machine Interaction Set – Volume 3)

HENROTIN Joseph
The Art of War in the Network Age
(Intellectual Technologies Set – Volume 1)

KITAJIMA Munéo
Memory and Action Selection in Human–Machine Interaction
(Human–Machine Interaction Set – Volume 1)

LAGRAÑA Fernando
E-mail and Behavioral Changes: Uses and Misuses of Electronic Communications

LEIGNEL Jean-Louis, UNGARO Thierry, STAAR Adrien
Digital Transformation
(Advances in Information Systems Set – Volume 6)

NOYER Jean-Max
Transformation of Collective Intelligences
(Intellectual Technologies Set – Volume 2)

VENTRE Daniel
Information Warfare – 2nd edition

VITALIS André
The Uncertain Digital Revolution
(Computing and Connected Society Set – Volume 1)

2015

ARDUIN Pierre-Emmanuel, GRUNDSTEIN Michel, ROSENTHAL-SABROUX Camille
Information and Knowledge System
(Advances in Information Systems Set – Volume 2)

BÉRANGER Jérôme
Medical Information Systems Ethics

BRONNER Gérald
Belief and Misbelief Asymmetry on the Internet

2013

BERNIK Igor
Cybercrime and Cyberwarfare

CAPET Philippe, DELAVALLADE Thomas
Information Evaluation

LEBRATY Jean-Fabrice, LOBRE-LEBRATY Katia
Crowdsourcing: One Step Beyond

SALLABERRY Christian
Geographical Information Retrieval in Textual Corpora

2012

BUCHER Bénédicte, LE BER Florence
Innovative Software Development in GIS

GAUSSIER Eric, YVON François
Textual Information Access

STOCKINGER Peter
Audiovisual Archives: Digital Text and Discourse Analysis

VENTRE Daniel
Cyber Conflict

2011

BANOS Arnaud, THÉVENIN Thomas
Geographical Information and Urban Transport Systems

DAUPHINÉ André
Fractal Geography

LEMBERGER Pirmin, MOREL Mederic
Managing Complexity of Information Systems

STOCKINGER Peter
Introduction to Audiovisual Archives

STOCKINGER Peter
Digital Audiovisual Archives

ROCHE Stéphane, CARON Claude
Organizational Facets of GIS

2008

BRUGNOT Gérard
Spatial Management of Risks

FINKE Gerd
Operations Research and Networks

GUERMOND Yves
Modeling Process in Geography

KANEVSKI Michael
Advanced Mapping of Environmental Data

MANOUVRIER Bernard, LAURENT Ménard
Application Integration: EAI, B2B, BPM and SOA

PAPY Fabrice
Digital Libraries

2007

DOBESCH Hartwig, DUMOLARD Pierre, DYRAS Izabela
Spatial Interpolation for Climate Data

SANDERS Lena
Models in Spatial Analysis

2006

CLIQUET Gérard
Geomarketing

CORNIOU Jean-Pierre
Looking Back and Going Forward in IT

DEVILLERS Rodolphe, JEANSOULIN Robert
Fundamentals of Spatial Data Quality

Printed and bound by CPI Group (UK) Ltd, Croydon, CR0 4YY